WRITING

ENGLISH in context

CAPITALIZATION AND PUNCTUATION

GRAMMAR AND USAGE

READING COMPREHENSION

SPELLING

VOCABULARY

WRITING

Development and Production: Laurel Associates, Inc.
Cover Art: Elisa Ligon

SADDLEBACK PUBLISHING, INC.
Three Watson
Irvine, CA 92618-2767

E-Mail: info@sdlback.com
Website: www.sdlback.com

ISBN 1-56254-358-X

Printed in the United States of America
05 04 03 02 01 00   9 8 7 6 5 4 3 2 1

CONTENTS

INTRODUCTION

Communication skills are crucial. People spend virtually all of their waking hours exercising one language arts skill or another. Experts have estimated that we spend 42 percent of our day listening, 32 percent of our day speaking, 15 percent of our day reading, and 11 percent writing.

While writing takes up the least of our time, it is by far the most complex and difficult language arts skill to master. Think about it. Since *writing is talk written down*, it involves remembering the sequence of sounds, the shapes of the letters, vocabulary, grammatical structures, and punctuation. To be a clear writer, you must first be a clear thinker.

Effective writing skills will help you in every area of your life—wherever you go and whatever you do! The exercises in this worktext teach "the basics" of good writing technique from the ground up. These techniques will reinforce skills you already have and suggest new and better ways to approach a writing assignment. In short, the work you are about to begin is well worth doing as patiently and carefully as you can. Why? Because increased competence will make all your future writing tasks so much easier!

EFFECTIVE WRITING: CONTENT AND FORM

UNIT 1

FOR HELP WITH GRAMMAR, CAPITALIZATION, PUNCTUATION, OR SPELLING, SEE THE REFERENCE GUIDE ON PAGES 112–128.

1 — FORM: CONTENT IN THE PROPER PACKAGE

There are two basic elements to any piece of writing. One is *content*—what the writer has to say. The other is *form*—the way the content, or message, is presented. The form of a written piece includes its organization and layout. Form gives a reader an immediate idea of what to expect. Without reading a word you could probably recognize a written piece by its form. A letter *looks like* a letter, an ad like an ad, an essay like an essay, a novel like a novel.

A

The items on the right are made up of nonsense letter groups. Using form as a clue, write a letter to match each item on the right with a type of communication named on the left.

1. _____ **poem**

2. _____ **friendly letter**

3. _____ **conversation**

4. _____ **paragraph**

a.
Xmxm Zxyxwvs,
   X vzwhk xm nvtrtzng. Wijwrm nrvink vr sklmplk xzyurst. Brggg flmzrx zsixxt stt. Trrrl frngzr clmp! Glrzzz frrr gbmlpzqr.
          Szzbmlp,
          Zrrrtship

b.
   Lgfr rjjklpt fdhbm fg zppprt vrfj zzwwqrt splt. Sqwww zzgrh brft ff, clp spbmklzzz vvbnm lpwqg. Zsdddvg hb ghfddd rwfr zzzvw qwwwt blppp nmgg. Crz bmpldffg zpp wwq vrghj klpqww.

c.
   "Splggfr wf grhqtt nwwz?" klggwd Brggz.
"Nz Slllkkzt frxxv dip?"
      "Gzzzlwrk skl tdddwq," trddid Mrgqk. "Jlkz!"

d.
Trug fligget mrik splinger con splan,
Wrik dugget mon brinker lon flan.
Pog wigget on plug,
Wrip stimet von slug,
Splig micket don wichet son blan.

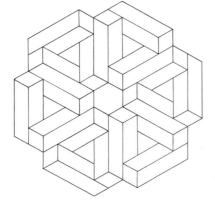

B

The activity on page 6 showed you form without content. This activity shows you content without form. Rewrite each item in its proper form.

1. Dear Joel, I can't believe it's your fifteenth birthday! Are you excited to get your learner's permit and begin driving? I'm sorry I can't visit, but you know it is harvest time on our farm. Hope you have a great birthday! Love, Aunt Amanda

   _____

   _____

   _____

   _____

   _____

2. Harvest Moon The first full moon of autumn is known as the Harvest Moon. It usually occurs around September 23 and rises at about the same time for several nights. The bright moonlight allows northern farmers to work in the fields late at night. They say the Harvest Moon is nature's gift.

   _____

   _____

   _____

   _____

   _____

   _____

C

Write _T_ or _F_ to tell whether each statement is _true_ or _false_.

1. _____ Proper form helps a reader separate main ideas.

2. _____ Form helps a reader recognize the writer's purpose.

3. _____ The proper form of a poem and a letter is the same.

4. _____ Form separates main parts of a written work.

5. _____ Form shows which person is speaking in a conversation.

6. _____ Proper form is only important in business writing and formal documents.

Proper form makes your message clearer. Good form is the mark of a good writer. Whenever you write, pay close attention to even margins, even spacing between words, and clearly indented paragraphs.

A

As you read this article, look for errors in form such as uneven margins, uneven spacing between words, and incorrectly indented paragraphs. Mark each error with a check (✓). The first error has been marked for you.

The Know-Nothings

✓ Between 1852 and 1860 a group of Americans turned a secret society into its own   political party. The party slogan was "Americans   must rule America," and the members had some unfair ideas. They   wanted to pass laws against electing foreign-born citizens or Catholics to public offices.   Theycalled themselvesthe American Party, but others called them the Know-Nothings.

   The Know-Nothings held secret meetings. They never told anyone what they discussed.   Whenever an outsider asked a question, a Know-Nothing would reply, "I don't know." This phrase gave the party its nickname.

B

The Know-Nothings had foolish ideas. Write a paragraph about a *good* idea for America. Make sure to do the following: write the title correctly; clearly indent the first line; keep even margins on both sides of the paper; and maintain even spacing between words and sentences.

_____

_____

_____

_____

_____

_____

Before you turn in a written work, take time to check form as well as content. Did you use the correct form for your purpose? Are the margins, indentations, and spaces even? Make sure you check your handwriting carefully. Did you cross *t*'s and dot *i*'s? Is it easy to tell an *o* from an *a* and an *n* from an *m*?

⟨A⟩

Carefully copy the paragraph in your best handwriting or printing.

The Loco-Focos

In 1835, a small group of New York Democrats earned a nickname. At a party meeting, the group brought up unpopular ideas about banking laws. Other Democrats would not listen! They blew out the lights and left the hall. The rebels relit the lanterns with a new type of match called the "loco-foco." The press quickly named the group the "Loco-Focos."

⟨B⟩

Use the following list to evaluate the paragraph you copied in Part A. Check the box as you review each item.

- [ ] I capitalized the title and centered it above the paragraph.
- [ ] I indented the first sentence of the paragraph.
- [ ] My left margin is exactly even.
- [ ] My right margin is nearly even.
- [ ] There are even spaces between words and sentences.
- [ ] I crossed all *t*'s and dotted all *i*'s.
- [ ] There is a clear difference between my *n*'s and *m*'s, *o*'s and *a*'s.
- [ ] It is clear that all sentences begin with a capital letter.
- [ ] There are correct punctuation marks at the ends of sentences.

BRAINSTORMING FOR CONTENT

Brainstorming is a good way to come up with content ideas for your writing. You can brainstorm alone, with a partner, or with a group. Suppose your teacher has assigned you to write a paragraph about a general topic. Your first job is to narrow the topic. Only a *specific* topic can be fully discussed in one paragraph. Brainstorming can help you explore possible ideas.

A general topic appears in the large center circle. Brainstorm related ideas and write them in the smaller circles. Some examples are shown.

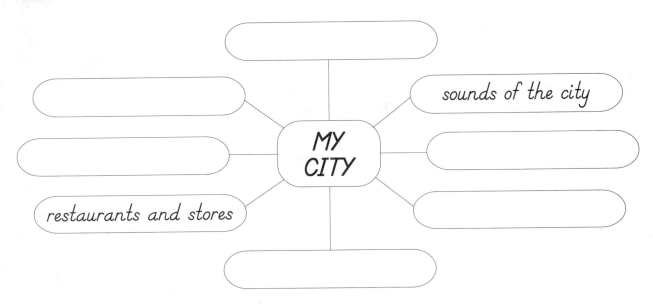

Once you have a specific topic, brainstorming can help you develop content. Select one topic from Part A. Write it in the center circle below. In the outer circles, write main ideas about that topic.

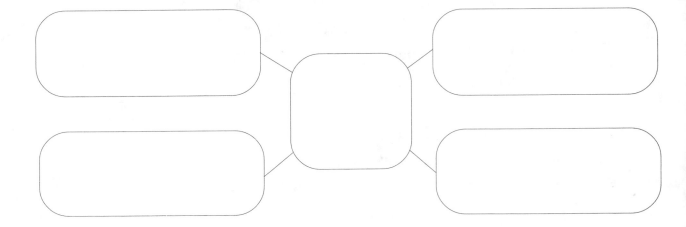

A Use the clues below to complete the puzzle.

ACROSS

3. the ideas in a piece of writing

4. the border along each side of a written piece

6. to complete the letter *i*

7. a technique for coming up with ideas

DOWN

1. the way something is written; its style and layout

2. to complete the letter *t*

5. to set the first line of a paragraph in from the margin

B Brainstorm four ideas you might include in a letter to a friend. Write your ideas in the outer circles.

Dear _____

C Use the ideas from Part B to write a letter to a friend. Use the checklist from page 9 to review your form.

_____

_____

_____

_____

_____

_____

SENTENCES

FOR HELP WITH GRAMMAR, CAPITALIZATION, PUNCTUATION, OR SPELLING, SEE THE REFERENCE GUIDE ON PAGES 112–128.

UNIT
2

 5 — ## COMPLETE SENTENCES: AVOIDING SENTENCE FRAGMENTS

A *complete sentence* must have a *subject* and a *predicate*. It must express a complete thought.

EXAMPLE: ***An orange cat*** ***rested on the sunny window sill***. (sentence)
　　　　　　　 SUBJECT　　　　　　　　　　 PREDICATE

A *sentence fragment* is a word group that begins with a capital letter and ends with an end mark but does *not* have both a subject and a predicate. Avoid this writing error in your own work.

EXAMPLE: ***An orange cat on the sunny window sill.*** (sentence fragment; no predicate)

A

Write *S* for *sentence* or *F* for *fragment* beside each group of words. Hint: You should find three fragments.

1. _____ Jumping beans grow in Central and South America.

2. _____ To jump and roll from side to side.

3. _____ The larva of a gypsy moth lives inside the bean.

4. _____ The larva moves about.

5. _____ The larva's movement makes the bean jump.

6. _____ Not an edible product.

7. _____ These beans from south of the border.

B

Rewrite each fragment from Part A as a complete sentence. You will have to add a subject or a predicate.

1. _____

2. _____

3. _____

C

Correct the sentence fragments. Either rewrite the fragment as a separate, complete sentence or make it part of another sentence. Use number one as a model.

1. The dingo is a wild dog of Australia. Howls like a wolf.

    The dingo is a wild dog of Australia that howls like a wolf.

2. Most dingoes have reddish-brown fur. Rough and coarse fur.

    _____

3. Long bushy tail. A dingo's face is like a wolf.

    _____

4. Dingoes always live in packs. Hunt sheep.

    _____

5. Many dingoes have been tamed. Guard their masters' sheep.

    _____

D

Write three complete sentences about any animal you know something about. Then use the checklist to make sure your sentences are correctly written.

1. _____

2. _____

3. _____

1	2	3	
☐	☐	☐	begins with a capital letter
☐	☐	☐	ends with a period, question mark, or exclamation point
☐	☐	☐	has a subject
☐	☐	☐	has a predicate
☐	☐	☐	expresses a complete thought

6 — COMPLETE SENTENCES: SEPARATING RUN-ON SENTENCES

When two or more sentences are incorrectly written as one sentence, the error is called a *run-on sentence*.

EXAMPLES: *The waiting room was packed with patients, an emergency had put the doctor behind schedule.* (run-on sentence)

The waiting room was packed with patients. An emergency had put the doctor behind schedule. (correctly separated sentence)

DID YOU NOTICE?

A comma cannot be used to separate two sentences. Each sentence must begin with a capital letter and end with a period, question mark, or exclamation point.

Correct these run-ons by writing two or three separate sentences.

1. Have you ever ridden a roller coaster was it a thrill?

   _____

   _____

2. In the 1400s some Russians carved sleds of ice they built ramps in the snow, these were the first roller coasters.

   _____

   _____

3. The French began building coasters in the early 1800s theirs had steel ramps and carts with wheels.

   _____

   _____

4. The first American coasters were not built as a thrill ride at all they were made for coal miners.

   _____

   _____

COMPOUND SUBJECTS AND PREDICATES 7

You may choose to write *compound subjects or predicates* to repair a sentence error or to avoid short, choppy sentences.

EXAMPLES:

SENTENCE FRAGMENT:
Roller coasters are popular amusement park rides. Merry-go-rounds too.

RUN-ON SENTENCE:
The coaster cars slowly climb the ramps, then they speed down them.

COMPLETE SENTENCE WITH COMPOUND SUBJECT:
Roller coasters and merry-go-rounds are popular amusement park rides.

COMPLETE SENTENCE WITH COMPOUND PREDICATE:
The coaster cars slowly climb the ramps and then speed down them.

 A

Some of these items contain sentence errors. Others are too short and choppy. Improve them by writing one sentence with a compound subject. The first one has been done as a model.

1. Roller coasters carry riders into the air. Ferris wheels too.

   Roller coasters and Ferris wheels carry riders into the air.

2. Japan has some of the biggest roller coasters and Ferris wheels. So does the United States.

   _____

   _____

3. "The Beast" is a giant coaster. "Moonsault Scramble" is another.

   _____

 B

Repair or improve each sentence by rewriting it as one sentence with a compound predicate.

1. George Ferris built the first amusement park wheel in 1893. He gave it his name.

   _____

   _____

2. Riders laugh. Riders scream. They come back for more.

   _____

8 — COMPOUND SENTENCES

A *compound sentence* consists of two sentences joined by a *coordinating conjunction*. You can write compound sentences to vary sentence lengths or to repair run-ons or fragments.

EXAMPLES:

TWO SEPARATE SENTENCES:

A snack of insects may not sound tasty to you. Some people eat bugs!

COMPOUND SENTENCE WITH COORDINATING CONJUNCTION:

A snack of insects may not sound tasty to you, but some people eat bugs!

SENTENCE FRAGMENT:

Snackers must choose their insect treats carefully. Could make themselves sick.

CORRECTLY WRITTEN COMPOUND SENTENCE:

Snackers must choose their insect treats carefully, or they could make themselves sick.

A

Join each pair of sentences with a comma and a coordinating conjunction (*and, but,* or *or*). Write the compound sentences on the lines.

1. Ice cream is a favorite treat. Cones are easy to eat on the run.

   _____

2. You may think of ice cream as an American treat. Italians invented it.

   _____

B

First write *fragment* or *run-on* to identify the error in each item. Then repair the error by writing a compound sentence on the line. Use the first item as a model.

1. Ice cream was once made only by expert chefs. Now a common dessert.

   fragment — *Ice cream was once made only by expert chefs, but now it is a common dessert.*

2. First lady Dolly Madison served ice cream. Only for special events.

   _____ — _____

   _____

3. Fans eat ice cream at ball games, children eat it at birthday parties.

   _____ — _____

   _____

Improving Sentences with Modifiers

Adjectives, adverbs, and prepositional phrases can help you combine or expand sentences.

EXAMPLE: ***The key turned in the lock. The key turned slowly.***
The lock was rusty. The key was iron. (original separate sentences)

The iron key turned slowly in the rusty lock. (combined sentence)
      ADJ.   ADV.   PREP. PHRASE

EXAMPLE: ***The door opened.*** (original sentence)

The heavy oak door slowly opened into the dungeon. (expanded sentence)
      ADJ. ADJ.   ADV.   PREP. PHRASE

Use adjectives, adverbs, and prepositional phrases to combine each set of sentences. Try to include all the information.

1. The berries are red. The berries are ripe. The berries are in Farmer Berg's field. The berries are ready to be picked.

   _____

2. The skier broke his leg. The skier was careless. The accident happened on his first run of the day. He was showing off.

   _____

B

Add adjectives, adverbs, and/or prepositional phrases to expand each sentence in two ways. First imagine a picture in your mind, and then help your reader to visualize it. The first one has been done for you.

1. A stranger appeared.
   a. *A smiling stranger in a red clown suit appeared at my door.*
   b. *A ghostly stranger dressed in white appeared in the clouds.*

2. A car passed.
   a. _____
   b. _____

3. The light flickered.
   a. _____
   b. _____

Sentences can be joined and improved by using *descriptive clauses*.

EXAMPLES:

SEPARATE SENTENCES:
James Madison was the shortest U.S. president.
He was five feet four inches tall.

COMPOUND SENTENCE WITH DESCRIPTIVE CLAUSE:
James Madison, who was five feet four inches tall,
was the shortest U.S. president.

A

Combine each pair of sentences into one complex sentence. Use a descriptive clause that begins with *who* or *which*. The first one has been done for you.

1. The final episode of *M*A*S*H* had the largest audience of any single program in TV history. It was first shown in 1983.

   *The final episode of M*A*S*H, which was first shown in 1983, had the largest audience of any show in TV history.*

2. Bill Cody was born in Wyoming. Wyoming is nicknamed the "Cowboy State."

   _____

   _____

3. Bill Cody once rode for the Pony Express. He later became known as Buffalo Bill.

   _____

   _____

4. The word *ramen* was recently added to the English dictionary. It names a type of quick-cooking noodles.

   _____

   _____

B

Finish each sentence by filling in the blanks and completing a descriptive clause.

1. My favorite TV show is _____, which

   _____.

2. Michael Jordan, who _____

_____, is one of the most famous people in the world.

3. I would like to say thank you to _____, who

_____.

You can also use *subordinating conjunctions* to form complex sentences and combine thoughts.

EXAMPLES:

SEPARATE SIMPLE SENTENCES:
Daffodils are planted in autumn.
They don't bloom until spring.

COMBINED COMPLEX SENTENCES WITH A SUBORDINATING CONJUNCTION:
Although daffodils are planted in fall,
they don't bloom until spring.
　　　—or—
Daffodils are planted in fall although
they don't bloom until spring.

DID YOU NOTICE?

When a subordinate clause comes at the beginning of a sentence, it is followed by a comma. When it comes at the end of a sentence, no comma is needed.

C

Use a subordinating conjunction from the box to combine each sentence pair into one complex sentence. Use the first item as a model.

SUBORDINATING CONJUNCTIONS					
after	although	because	before	if	since
unless	until	when	whenever	while	

1. The daddy longlegs looks scary. It is a harmless spider.
   Although the daddy longlegs looks scary, it is a harmless spider.

2. The cat is sometimes away. That is when the mice will play.

   _____

3. Sometimes I eat strawberries too often. I get a rash.

   _____

4. Romeo thought Juliet was dead. He drank poison.

   _____

11 COMBINING AND REPAIRING SENTENCES

Do your sentences sound choppy? Do you write fragments or run-ons? You can repair these kinds of errors by writing compound subjects and predicates, compound sentences, or complex sentences.

A

Follow the directions to combine each pair of sentences. Use the first item as a model.

1. Rock and roll star Buddy Holly was killed in a plane crash. Rock and roll stars Richie Valens and The Big Bopper died in the same crash. **(Write one sentence with a compound subject.)**

   Rock and roll stars Buddy Holly, Richie Valens, and The Big Bopper were killed in a plane crash.

2. Three great musicians died on that winter night. Fans called it "the night the music died." **(Use a subordinating conjunction to form one complex sentence.)**

   _____

   _____

3. Ricky Nelson died in a later plane crash. He was also a rock star. **(Write one complex sentence with a descriptive clause.)**

   _____

   _____

4. Fans haven't forgotten these musicians. They still play their songs. **(Write one sentence with a compound predicate.)**

   _____

   _____

5. These singers died at young ages. Their music changed rock and roll. **(Use a coordinating conjunction to form one compound sentence.)**

   _____

   _____

B

The following paragraph has many short, choppy sentences. It also contains a sentence fragment and a run-on sentence. As you rewrite the paragraph, combine some of the sentences and repair the errors.

It was the year 2000. Harold was a rich man. He was very sick. He arranged to have himself frozen. Just before he died. He remained frozen for a long time. Some 300 years went by someone thawed Harold out. Harold opened his eyes. He saw a new world.

_____

_____

_____

_____

_____

_____

C

Write a paragraph describing the world Harold might have found when he awoke in 2300. Vary your sentence structure to avoid short, choppy sentences. Avoid fragments and run-ons.

_____

_____

_____

_____

_____

_____

_____

12 — TIGHTENING OVERWRITTEN SENTENCES

A long piece of writing is not necessarily a good one. Using unnecessary words and repeating thoughts are common writing mistakes. Compare the example sentences. Look for words that repeat meaning and add unnecessary information in the first sentence. Notice that the shorter sentence is clear and direct.

EXAMPLE: *Many artists, sculptors, and painters live on the Left Bank of the French city of Paris, France.* (overwritten sentence)

Many artists live on the Left Bank of Paris. (tightened sentence)

A

Cross out repeated or unnecessary words and word groups in each sentence. Use the first item as a model.

1. Her shoes ~~on her feet~~ were too tight ~~and fit poorly~~.

2. I am having a hard time with the exam's difficult test questions.

3. The railway train raced swiftly down the railroad tracks.

4. The basketball player looked like a huge giant in the kindergarten students' class.

B

Rewrite each sentence, leaving out words that repeat information.

1. The French word "bonjour" is a welcoming greeting that the French people use to say hello.

   _____

2. I visited France as a tourist in the year 1992.

   _____

3. Two twin French girls showed me the attractions and sights.

   _____

4. They explained and told me how France had won freedom and liberty during the revolution.

   _____

5. We sat out on the sidewalk at a sidewalk cafe and watched people walk and stroll by.

_____

6. I hope to go back and revisit Paris some future day.

_____

C

Simplify the following phrases and clauses. The first one has been done for you.

1. the girl with the blue eyes = *the blue-eyed girl*

2. the car that is speeding = _____

3. the employees who work hard = _____

4. the sandwich that is stale = _____

5. the room in the attic = _____

D

Make the following paragraph shorter, clearer, and more direct. Remove unnecessary words and reduce the number of phrases and clauses.

> Beings who are human have long been fascinated by dreams since the beginning of time. People's dreams seem to have similar themes and topics which are alike. Did you ever dream you were flying up above the ground? This dream, which is common, may show a desire for freedom and independence from the problems and troubles of life.

_____

_____

_____

_____

_____

_____

13 USING PRECISE AND DESCRIPTIVE WORDS

Adjectives can create colorful images for a reader. A writer might expand the phrase "a man" to say "a tall, distinguished man." Good writers send a descriptive message with nouns and verbs, too. "The tall, distinguished *gentleman*" paints an even more colorful picture. Precise, descriptive nouns and verbs are powerful tools for creating clear images.

A

For numbers 1–12, circle the noun or verb that creates the clearest image. For numbers 13–18, add a more specific noun or verb to create a clearer image.

1. eat / nibble

2. make / assemble

3. rain / downpour

4. bite / sting

5. cat / tabby

6. giggle / laugh

7. cry / weep

8. nag / horse

9. party / festival

10. bird / crow

11. sing / warble

12. walk / stroll

13. house / _____

14. talk / _____

15. ask / _____

16. snake / _____

17. run / _____

18. job / _____

B

Read the paragraph below. Replace each noun or verb in parentheses with a word that creates a clearer image.

As soon as I awoke, I knew this would

be a **(bad)** _____ day. Rain

(hit) _____ my window.

The wind **(blew)** _____.

I **(got)** _____ out of bed and

(walked) _____ into the bathroom. I turned on the

faucet. Just one drop of cold water **(came)** _____ out.

My **(dog)** _____, Curly, **(looked)** _____

at me from where he **(was)** _____ on the floor. He seemed

to say, "Just stay in bed!"

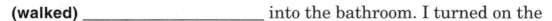

A Each item below contains a writing problem. Write a letter to match each item with one of the problems listed in the box.

a. sentence fragment	b. run-on sentence	c. repetition

1. _____ We visited New Orleans, we stayed in the French Quarter.

2. _____ We listened to jazz music on a street called Bourbon Street.

3. _____ New Orleans is known for its Creole food. Also Cajun dishes.

B Rewrite each item in Part A as one correct sentence.

1. _____

2. _____

3. _____

C The following quote was written as a run-on sentence. Follow the directions to repair the run-on in four different ways.

> *Some books make me want to go adventuring, others save me the trouble.* —Ashleigh Brilliant

Rewrite the quote:

1. **as two separate sentences.** _____
   _____

2. **by using a coordinating conjunction to form a compound sentence.** _____
   _____
   _____

3. **as one simple sentence with a compound predicate.** _____
   _____
   _____

4. **by using a subordinating conjunction to form a complex sentence.** _____
   _____
   _____

PARAGRAPHS

FOR HELP WITH GRAMMAR, CAPITALIZATION, PUNCTUATION, OR SPELLING, SEE THE REFERENCE GUIDE ON PAGES 112–128.

UNIT
3

14 STATING THE PARAGRAPH TOPIC

A paragraph is made up of a *topic sentence* and a body of *detail sentences*. Usually, a paragraph that stands alone has a *concluding sentence*. The topic sentence states the main idea. Most often it is the first sentence. All detail sentences support, or relate to, the idea expressed in the topic sentence.

A

Find and underline the topic sentence in each paragraph below.

1. It is surprising how many companies have used a dog as a trademark. Since 1902, ads have shown the Boston terrier Tige with his master, Buster Brown. Many Americans recall RCA's Nipper, the terrier who sat in front of an old gramophone. The sleek greyhound of Greyhound Bus Lines is another well-remembered trademark. Trademark dogs still appear regularly in commercials and on product labels.

2. The term "bookworm" usually describes someone who reads a lot. There are, however, *real* bookworms. These are insect larvae that feed on the paste in book bindings. They are sometimes found in dusty bookstores and libraries.

B

The following paragraph has no topic sentence. Circle the letter of the appropriate topic sentence below the paragraph.

Some nicknames express disapproval. When Andrew Johnson vetoed 22 bills, his foes called him "Sir Veto." Other names show admiration. For example, President Martin Van Buren's clever politics earned him the title "the Fox." George Washington was impressively nicknamed "Father of Our Country." Jimmy Carter, who ran a Georgia peanut farm, was casually known as the "Peanut President."

a. The United States has had some great leaders.

b. Most American presidents have had nicknames.

c. America's presidents come from many backgrounds.

C

Read the two topic sentences. Then read the detail sentences listed below them. Write the letter of each detail on a line beside the topic sentence it supports.

1. _____, _____, _____   **Americans drink more coffee than people of any other nation.**

2. _____, _____, _____   **Coffee has some strong effects on the human body.**

a. The average American drinks about 16 pounds of coffee a year.

b. The caffeine in coffee can increase blood pressure.

c. Drinking large amounts of coffee can lead to nervousness, sleeplessness, or stomach problems.

d. The United States uses nearly two-thirds of the world's coffee.

e. Even when the price of beans rises sharply, few Americans give up their morning coffee.

f. Some people say that coffee helps them feel alert.

D

The paragraph below lacks a topic sentence. Read the body of the paragraph. Then return to the beginning and write a topic sentence.

_____

_____

_____. Some cacti grow as low bushes. Others grow like vines. One variety is called the "old man" cactus because its stiff white hairs look like whiskers. Another has large white flowers that open only at night. While most people think of cacti as prickly plants, some varieties have no spines at all.

15 — SUPPORTING SENTENCES

Remember: The body of a paragraph contains detail sentences that support the topic sentence. A strong paragraph needs at least three detail sentences. To evaluate your paragraphs, ask yourself: *Do all the sentences in the body relate to the main idea? Do they support the point made in the topic sentence?*

A

Read the paragaraph. Then underline the topic sentence, and cross out the one sentence that does not support the topic sentence.

At times I feel like my dog is the master and I am his pet. At 8:00 each morning he barks to say that he expects a walk. I jump at his command and hurry to fetch the leash. At 5:00 each evening he stands before his dish. I hurry to fill it. Humans on every continent in the world have kept dogs as pets. My dog has taught me to be a faithful and loyal companion. I must say, my dog is lucky to own me!

B

First fill in the blank to complete the topic sentence. Then write three sentences that support the idea expressed in the topic sentence.

TOPIC SENTENCE: I think I could be a great _____.

SUPPORTING SENTENCES:

1. _____

   _____

2. _____

   _____

3. _____

   _____

A paragraph's *concluding sentence* helps a reader recall the main idea and recognize the point that has been made. Usually, the concluding sentence summarizes the information but does not add new details. It often rephrases the idea expressed in the topic sentence (expresses it in different words). When a paragraph stands alone and is not part of a larger piece of writing, it usually has a concluding sentence.

A

Read the paragraph. Circle the letter of the best conclusion.

A U.S. naval unit called the Seabees helped win World War II. The Seabees were trained not to fight but to build. When the United States needed air bases in the Pacific, the Seabees went to work. With the motto, "Can do!" they worked to clear island jungles. They built bridges, airstrips, roads, and hospitals. Their battalions constructed floating docks so ships could quickly unload equipment.

   a. On February 19, 1945, marines landed on the island of Iwo Jima.

   b. Fighting in the Pacific continued after the war in Europe ended.

   c. The Seabees paved the way to victory for U.S. fighting forces.

   d. I think I will make my own motto "Can do!"

B

Write a concluding sentence for this paragraph.

American kids did their part during World War II. They went from door to door on scrap drives. The old newspapers, rubber, tin cans, and bits of metal they collected were recycled for the war effort. Children spent their hard-earned coins on War Stamps and saved the stamps to trade for War Bonds. In all, America's youth spent more than $100 million on War Stamps. The money bought airplanes, jeeps, and other equipment. _____

_____.

17 TRANSITIONAL WORDS

Transitional words connect sentences by showing how ideas are related. Read the transitional words in the box. Think about how they could link sentences and guide the reader through a paragraph.

as a result	on the other hand	however	finally	then
in addition	in comparison	therefore	indeed	first
in conclusion	in other words	in fact	also	thus
for example	then again	although	next	

Circle the transitional words that most clearly show the relationship between each pair of sentences.

1. Tommy is quiet and studious. (Furthermore / However), his twin brother Timmy is noisy and active.

2. Tommy studies harder than Timmy. (As a result / On the other hand), Tommy usually gets A's while Timmy is lucky to pass.

3. Home remedies can actually make sick people feel better. (For example / In conclusion), the hot liquid in chicken soup may reduce cold symptoms.

4. Consider all the possibilities before you decide to undertake a new endeavor. (In other words / Thus), *look before you leap*.

5. First bait the fishhook. (Then / Therefore) cast the line into the water.

Underline the transitional words in the following paragraph.

In his farewell address, George Washington gave some warnings. First, he cautioned that the United States might someday become divided. In addition, he warned that people might be more loyal to their party than to their country. Washington also advised Americans to keep out of other countries' wars. Many of the problems that Washington foresaw have, indeed, troubled our nation.

FACTUAL PARAGRAPHS

A *factual paragraph* provides the reader with information. Its topic sentence may include a definition, such as this: *The chipmunk is a small, furry animal that belongs to the rodent family.* An informational paragraph develops the topic with facts.

A

Think about each topic below. Then write a definition that could be the topic sentence of a factual paragraph. You may use a dictionary or encyclopedia if you need help.

1. **Sitting Bull:** _____

   _____

2. **laser:** _____

   _____

B

Use the following notes to write a factual paragraph. Be sure to write a topic sentence. It is not necessary to include *all* the facts.

a. orangutan, giant ape from Sumatra and Borneo

b. name means "wild man"

c. lives in groups no larger than family group

d. nests on platforms 25 feet above ground

e. four to five feet high

f. coarse, red-brown hair

g. highest forehead of all apes

h. very long arms

i. swings from branch to branch

j. prefers eating vegetables

_____

_____

_____

_____

_____

_____

_____

_____

19 SUMMARY PARAGRAPHS

At times you may need to *summarize* a long piece of writing. To summarize, you will pick out only the most important points. A summary does not include minor or unimportant details.

A

Read the following selection. Underline the details you consider most important.

ELLIS ISLAND

Ellis Island, a man-made island in New York Harbor, was a U.S. immigration station for more than 60 years. Between 1892 and 1952, it was known as the "Door to the United States." Most newcomers to America during those years had to come through Ellis Island. During that time, more than 20 million people came from all over the world, mostly from the countries of Europe.

New immigrants received medical exams at Ellis Island. If they were sick, they were not allowed to enter the United States. They had to return to their homeland. Immigrants were also carefully questioned. Officers asked, "Do you have relatives in the United States? Do you have a place to stay? Is there a job waiting for you?"

Ellis Island was a frightening place for many immigrants. Most of them spoke no English. They were strangers in a new land. Their concern about the unknown mingled with the worry that they would be turned away. The immigrants' fears and disappointments prompted Ellis Island to be called the "Island of Tears."

B

Write a paragraph summarizing the article from Part A. Begin with a topic sentence that states the main idea.

_____

_____

_____

_____

_____

_____

_____

_____

One way to organize paragraph details is in *chronological* or *time order*. This is a logical way to tell how to do something or describe an event from beginning to end.

 A

The sentences below are out of time order. Write letters on the numbered lines in the box to put the sentences in chronological order. The first one has been done for you.

> 1. _c_   2. _____   3. _____   4. _____   5. _____   6. _____   7. _____

a. I tiptoed down the stairs.

b. At the bottom of the stairs, I could hear noises in the kitchen.

c. A strange, tapping sound woke me from a deep sleep.

d. I shined my flashlight across the kitchen floor.

e. I swung open the kitchen door.

f. A mouse wearing tap shoes clicked its heels and smiled.

g. I climbed out of bed and took a flashlight from a bedside drawer.

B

Use the sentences from Part A to write a paragraph in time order. Select at least two transitional words from the box below and use them in your paragraph. They will help your reader follow the time order.

first	then	next	later	finally	right then	in the next minute

_____

_____

_____

_____

_____

_____

_____

21 — DESCRIPTIVE PARAGRAPHS

A *descriptive paragraph* aims to present details to a reader as clearly as possible. When it stands alone, a descriptive paragraph usually has a concluding sentence. The concluding sentence summarizes the topic and may express the writer's feelings about it.

A

You can't write a complete description if your topic is too broad. Narrow each topic below to one that would be appropriate for a single paragraph. The first one has been done as a model.

1. **autumn:** *the colors of autumn leaves*

2. **relatives:** _____

3. **teachers:** _____

4. **basketball:** _____

5. **fads:** _____

6. **storms:** _____

B

Choose one of the topics you wrote in Part A. Plan a descriptive paragraph by filling in the blanks.

1. TOPIC: _____

2. TOPIC SENTENCE: _____

   _____

3. FIRST DETAIL SENTENCE: _____

   _____

4. SECOND DETAIL SENTENCE: _____

   _____

5. THIRD DETAIL SENTENCE: _____

   _____

6. CONCLUDING SENTENCE: _____

   _____

When you write a descriptive paragraph, think about the old saying, "actions speak louder than words." Suppose you are describing real people or literary characters. You can strengthen your descriptive words with examples of things the character has done or said. If you describe someone as "generous," back up the comment. Tell about a generous act.

C

For this exercise, first think of people or literary characters that you feel strongly about. Then fill in the blanks. Use No. 1 as a model.

1. a. PERSON/CHARACTER: _my cousin Richie_

   b. DESCRIPTIVE WORD: _conceited_

   c. SOMETHING HE/SHE DID OR SAID THAT SUPPORTS THE DESCRIPTIVE WORD: _When we were going to a party, Richie said to let him go in first so everyone would think we were cool._

2. a. PERSON/CHARACTER: _____

   b. DESCRIPTIVE WORD: _____

   c. SOMETHING HE/SHE DID OR SAID THAT SUPPORTS THE DESCRIPTIVE WORD: _____

   _____

   _____

   _____

3. a. PERSON/CHARACTER: _____

   b. DESCRIPTIVE WORD: _____

   c. SOMETHING HE/SHE DID OR SAID THAT SUPPORTS THE DESCRIPTIVE WORD: _____

   _____

   _____

   _____

22 — PERSUASIVE PARAGRAPHS

The topic sentence of a *persuasive paragraph* makes the subject clear and states your opinion about it. The body of the paragraph gives reasons and facts to convince a reader to agree with you. The conclusion restates your opinion.

A

Write a sentence expressing your opinion on each subject.

1. **fast foods in school cafeterias:** _____
   _____

2. **required driver's education classes:** _____
   _____

3. **school uniforms:** _____
   _____

4. **students and part-time jobs:** _____
   _____

5. **pop quizzes:** _____
   _____

6. **homework:** _____
   _____

B

Choose one of your sentences from Part A. Using it as a topic sentence, write a paragraph to persuade a reader that your opinion is right.

_____

_____

_____

_____

_____

_____

_____

_____

Selling something always involves persuasion. Whether you are selling your old bike, a new idea, or yourself as an employee, you will want to present the strongest reasons you can.

C

Complete each sentence. List three reasons that might persuade your reader to accept your opinion.

1. I think you would enjoy owning this _____.

   a. _____

   b. _____

   c. _____

2. I believe I should be hired as a _____

   at your _____.

   a. _____

   b. _____

   c. _____

3. As a teacher, I think you should consider my suggestion to _____

   _____.

   a. _____

   b. _____

   c. _____

D

Write a persuasive paragraph based on a topic from Part C.

_____

_____

_____

_____

_____

_____

_____

PARAGRAPHS OF COMPARISON

A *paragraph of comparison* tells how two things are alike or different. The topic sentence presents two subjects and sets up the comparison. The body gives details of similarities or differences. The concluding sentence restates the subjects being compared. Use transitional words such as *similarly* and *in comparison* to clue readers that you are presenting similarities. Use words like *on the other hand* and *however* to suggest differences.

A

Put a check (✓) beside the topic sentences that suggest the writer is beginning a paragraph of comparison.

1. _____ The *Dunkly Daily* and *Midcity Monitor* are both fine newspapers.

2. _____ The years 1899 and 1999 had several things in common.

3. _____ The fierce tornado of 1999 left thousands homeless.

4. _____ The television ad for Slipperino Soap is a work of art.

B

Use a diagram to brainstorm similarities and differences. First study the model. Note that it lists the unique features of two subjects in the outer sections and similarities in the center, intersecting section. Now complete a diagram comparing two subjects of your choice.

Topics: **SUPERMARKET**   *SIMILARITIES*   **SPECIALTY STORE**

- one-stop shopping
- lowest prices
- varying quality
- owned by corporation
- open long hours

- many brands
- helpful clerks
- easy returns

- personal service
- higher prices
- high-quality goods
- owner works in store
- limited hours

Topics: _____   *SIMILARITIES*   _____

- _____
  _____

- _____
  _____

- _____
  _____

- _____
  _____

- _____
  _____

- _____
  _____

- _____
  _____

- _____
  _____

- _____
  _____

A Write a letter in the blank to match each topic sentence to the type of paragraph it would likely introduce.

> 1. _____ factual paragraph
>
> 2. _____ summary paragraph
>
> 3. _____ time-order paragraph
>
> 4. _____ descriptive paragraph
>
> 5. _____ persuasive paragraph
>
> 6. _____ comparative paragraph

a. The sun-tanned vaquero rode across the open prairie.

b. This nation's first cowboys were the Mexican vaqueros.

c. The article, "Vaqueros: The First Cowboys," explains the historic role of the Hispanic vaqueros.

d. Hispanic cowboys and Anglo cowboys did similar work but received different treatment.

e. In my opinion, history does not give enough credit to the Hispanic vaquero.

f. There are five difficult and dangerous steps to roping a bull.

B Write a topic sentence for the following list of supporting details.

TOPIC SENTENCE: _____

_____

DETAILS:

1. In his 18 years with the Pittsburgh Pirates, Roberto Clemente won four batting championships.

2. He played in 12 all-star games.

3. Clemente held a lifetime batting average of .317.

4. Many teammates and managers called him the greatest baseball player they had ever seen.

REWRITING: PROOFREADING AND REVISING

FOR HELP WITH GRAMMAR, CAPITALIZATION, PUNCTUATION, OR SPELLING, SEE THE REFERENCE GUIDE ON PAGES 112–128.

UNIT
4

24 — USING STANDARD PROOFREADER'S MARKS

Proofreading means looking for mistakes or problems in a piece of writing. *Revising* means correcting errors and making changes. The standard proofreader's marks on this chart show common revisions.

PROOFREADING MARKS

Mark	Meaning	Example
¶	Indent to begin paragraph.	¶ *I think dogs dream. When Fido sleeps, he makes odd noises.*
≡	Change to a capital letter.	*my dog seems to dream.*
/	Change to a small letter.	*My Mom is an engineer.*
⊙	Insert a period.	*I love pizza⊙*
∧	Insert a comma.	*Sam, please shut the door.*
∩	Reverse the order.	*I voted for Walt.*
⌒	Close this space.	*Watch out for wet roads.*
∧	Insert anything missing.	*We drove to the west end of town.*
ℓ	Omit something.	*I ate a giant-sized huge taco.*
⌣ ⌣	Add quotation marks.	*Margo asked, Where is the exit?*
⌣	Add an apostrophe.	*This is Ginas car.*

A

Use the revisions marked to help you rewrite each sentence correctly. Refer to the chart for help in recognizing the proofreader's marks.

1. The most common last name in the world is not Johnson or jones⊙

_____

2. Its the chinese name Chang.

_____

3. About almost 12 percent of Chinese People, or at least 104 million individauls use that surname.

_____

4. "My last name is Smith," said Walter. "That is the most common last name in tᴐhe united states."

_____

5. "There are more than two miłion smiths in the united states," he continued.

_____

B

Use proofreader's marks to make revisions on the paragraph below. Then rewrite the paragraph correctly.

The Hula Hoop was one of the biggest fads ever to sweep the United states. Wham-O introduced the Hula Hoop in the 1950s. The craze began when a company executive was given a bamboo exercise hoop from india. Wham-O quickly began making plastic versions of the Hoop. everybody loved them. The public bought 25 million Hula Hoops within the first four months of production. Before the year was up Americans of all all ages were spining the hoops for fun for exercise and in competitions. Wham-O had found the super-toy of the the Decade

_____
_____
_____
_____
_____
_____
_____
_____
_____
_____

A

Each of these proverbs contains three writing errors. Use the proofreader's marks on page 40 to make corrections. Use the first sentence as a model.

1. some have been thought brave because they were afraid to run away. *(Russia)*

2. Those who keep company wiht a Wolf will learn to howl   *(England)*

3. every fool want's too give advice.   *(Italy)*

4. Its needless to pour water on a   drowned Mouse.   *(England)*

5. Life is the greattest bargain. we get it for nothing   *(Yiddish)*

6. be patient In time even an Egg will walk.   *(African)*

7. Love a cough and an itch cant be hid.   *(Unknown)*

8. If we didnt have ordinary men How could we tell who the great ones are?   *(Japan)*

B

Rewrite the proverbs from Part A correctly.

1. _____

_____

2. _____

3. _____

4. _____

5. _____

6. _____

7. _____

8. _____

_____

Proofreaders must constantly be on the lookout for misspelled words.

 A

Proofread the following limerick for spelling. Draw a neat line through each misspelled word. Then write the correct spelling above it. (You may use a dictionary for help.) Finally, rewrite the limerick correctly.

There is a new gurl in home room,

Who wares a sweet smelling purfoom.

When there is a breeze,

You'll heer sneeze after sneeze,

She's like a spring gardin in bloom.

PERFUME

_____

_____

_____

_____

_____

B

Find 10 misspelled words in the following paragraph. Draw a line through each one. Then write the correct spelling above the word.

During colonial days, last names often came from famly occupations. The popular names Taylor and Mason, for exampul, named trades. A "tailor" made clothing and a "mason" laid bricks. In the Dutch colonys, clay bricks were called _knickers_, and the persun who baked them was the _knicker baker_. The name, later changed to Knickerbocker, became verry common among Dutch settilers. Even today, evry U.S. telefone book lists many names that were originly occupashuns.

27 — PROOFREADING FOR ORGANIZATION AND CONTENT

A

Select a nonfiction paragraph you have already written. It might come from a Unit 3 activity or be part of a class report. If you prefer, you may write a new paragraph about one of the following: (a) an accident, (b) a personal victory, (c) a historical figure, or (d) a public facility that would improve your city. Write your paragraph below.

_____

_____

_____

_____

_____

_____

_____

_____

_____

_____

_____

B

Now proofread your paragraph to check organization and content. Then answer each question with *yes* or *no*.

1. _____ Did you indent your paragaraph?

2. _____ Does your paragraph have a topic sentence that presents its main idea?

3. _____ Does each sentence in the body of your paragraph support the main idea?

4. _____ Does each sentence express a complete thought?

5. _____ Is your main idea supported by at least three detail sentences?

6. _____ Do transitional words guide the reader and connect some of the ideas?

7. _____ Does a concluding sentence restate the main point?

A

Rewrite your paragraph from Lesson 27.
Correct any problems you had with
organization and/or content. Write in
your best handwriting.

_____

_____

_____

_____

_____

_____

_____

_____

_____

_____

_____

B

Now proofread your rewritten paragraph for punctuation, spelling,
and other writing mechanics. Use proofreader's marks to show your
revisions. As you proofread, check off each item listed below. Turn
to the Reference Guide in the back of the book if you need help.

☐ complete sentences

☐ spelling

☐ punctuation

☐ capitalization of proper names

☐ subject-verb agreement

☐ pronouns and antecedents

☐ plurals and possessives

☐ parallel construction

☐ uniform verb tense

29 PROOFREADING FOR CONSISTENCY

Before handing in written work, make sure that important sentence and paragraph elements agree. As you proofread your writing, check for these common consistency problems.

- *shifts from present tense to past tense*

    EXAMPLES: Flies **landed** on the horse. The horse **flicks** them with his tail. (incorrect)

PAST ――――――― PRESENT

    Flies **landed** on the horse. The horse **flicked** them with his tail. (correct)

PAST ――――――― PAST

- *agreement in number*

    EXAMPLES: If **girls** wear too much makeup, **she** will look like a clown. (incorrect)

PLURAL ――――――― SINGULAR

    If **girls** wear too much makeup, **they** will look like clowns. (correct)

PLURAL ――――――― PLURAL

- *shifts in pronoun reference*

    EXAMPLES: **Athletes** need a healthy diet. **You** should avoid too much candy. (incorrect)

THIRD PERSON ――――――― SECOND PERSON

    Athletes need a healthy diet. **They** should avoid too much candy. (correct)

THIRD PERSON ――――――― THIRD PERSON

Rewrite the sentences to correct consistency problems.

1. If students forget their homework, he should get a second chance.

    _____

    _____

2. He always works on Mondays. He played golf on Tuesdays.

    _____

    _____

3. A mountain climber must use caution with every step you take.

    _____

    _____

Redundant sentences contain unnecessary or repetitive words. Redundant paragraphs include repeated details. Proofread to be sure that each word and each sentence in your paragraph adds something new.

Rewrite the following sentences. Eliminate any repeated details or ideas.

Many colonists came to America in search of freedom of religion. They wanted self-government and the right to worship freely.

_____

_____

B

The following paragraph is loaded with repeated ideas. Rewrite the paragraph and its title. Try to cut the paragraph to five sentences by eliminating redundancy.

> ### My Own Opinion on Modesty
>
> I think modesty is, in my opinion, a very fine quality. I like people who don't act like they are really great or important. Every single person in this whole wide world is important and valuable, and I think that a really good person recognizes this and is modest. For example, I admire famous and well-known athletes and stars who take time to thank their fans and who appreciate the people who pay money to see them. It is important for a person to have self-confidence and feel capable of doing things well. However, it takes a certain amount of a quality called modesty to keep self-confidence from turning into conceit. There is a difference between being self-confident and having a swollen head and a big ego. So, in my opinion, I like modest people.

_____

_____

_____

_____

_____

_____

_____

31 — THE FINAL COPY

Check off each step as you complete it.

☐ Read your rewritten paragraph from Lesson 28 aloud. *Listen* for any awkward phrases or errors.

☐ Make any corrections you think necessary.

☐ Have someone else read your paragraph and offer suggestions for improvement.

B

A good writer must also be his or her own critic. *You* must be satisfied with the final copy before you present to your reader. Write a sentence or two explaining what you like about your paragraph.

_____

_____

_____

C

Write the final version of your paragraph here.

_____

_____

_____

_____

_____

_____

_____

_____

_____

_____

UNIT REVIEW 4

A Study the symbols in the box. Then match each proofreader's mark with the instruction it gives.

> 1. ____ ⌄   2. ____ ≡   3. ____ ⌿   4. ____ ⊙   5. ____ ⋏   6. ____ ∩

a. Insert a comma.

b. Change to a capital letter.

c. Omit something.

d. Insert an apostrophe.

e. Insert a period.

f. Reverse the order.

B Rewrite the quotation on the lines. Use the proofreader's marks to correct it.

> ≡what is i̶s̶ written with⌒out effort is in ̷General re͟a͟d with⌒out pleasure⊙
>
> —Samuel Johnson

_____

_____

C Proofread the following sentences. Use the proofreader's marks on page 40 to show the necessary revisions. Use the ⌿ mark to delete any redundant words and ideas.

1. Levi Strauss arived in San Francisco in the month of march 1853

2. "gold miners are sure to need thread needles scissors, and canvas cloth, Strauss told his brother jonas.

3. He loaded his goods and wares on a cart and wheeled them through San Franciscos Streets.

4. "Do you have any pants to sell? an old elderly Prospector asked. I cant find a pair of pants that will last!"

5. Strauss quickly found a Tailor and created first original pair of jeans.

6. levi's sturdy pants were instantly a immediate hit

49

WRITING TO EXPLAIN OR INFORM

FOR HELP WITH GRAMMAR, CAPITALIZATION, PUNCTUATION, OR SPELLING, SEE THE REFERENCE GUIDE ON PAGES 112–128.

UNIT **5**

32 — WRITING FOR A PURPOSE

Before you begin to write, think about your purpose. Ask yourself, *What am I trying to do for my reader?* Often, your aim will be to provide information by explaining or describing. Remember these hints when writing to inform:

- Keep your purpose clearly in mind.
- Make your topic narrow enough to allow a full explanation or description.
- Write a topic sentence that clarifies your topic and purpose.
- Use strong, specific words to create sharp images.
- If possible, involve several of your reader's senses.

A

Read the following topic sentences. Which sentences suggest that the writer will explain or describe something? Put a check (✓) by those sentences.

1. _____ A squall is a short, violent storm.

2. _____ Join me for a visit to a Mexican hacienda.

3. _____ The platypus is a small Australian water animal.

4. _____ It was midnight when the stranger knocked at our door.

5. _____ In my opinion, physical education should be a required subject.

B

Which topics below are narrow enough for one explanatory or descriptive paragraph? Circle five topics.

1. mountains of the Americas

2. Uncle Willie's weird invention

3. a knight's suit of armor

4. a hailstorm to remember

5. musical instruments

6. the kumquat

7. the Middle Ages

8. my relatives

9. the bear cub

10. fruit

C

For each listed word, write two words that are more specific and descriptive. Use the first item as a model.

1. drink

    gulp

    sip

2. laugh

    _____

    _____

3. carry

    _____

    _____

D

Describe one of the following places or things to an imaginary visitor from outer space: (a) the monkey house at the zoo, (b) a garbage dump, (c) a roller coaster, or (d) an erupting volcano. First visualize the topic and then write a definition of it. Finally, answer the questions.

1. DEFINITION: _____

2. WHAT DO YOU SEE? _____

3. WHAT DO YOU HEAR? _____

4. WHAT DO YOU SMELL? _____

5. WHAT MIGHT YOU TOUCH? _____

6. HOW DOES IT MAKE YOU FEEL? _____

    _____

7. WHAT ONE DETAIL ABOUT THE THING STANDS OUT IN YOUR MIND? _____

    _____

E

Imagine that your reader is someone who has never left home. Write a paragraph explaining or describing one of the following: (a) *snow* to someone from the tropics, (b) the *ocean* to someone from the Midwest, (c) a rush hour *traffic jam* to someone from a rural area, or (d) a forested *campsite* to a city dweller.

_____

_____

_____

_____

_____

_____

EXPLAINING HOW TO GET THERE

Pretend that you are on a corner waiting for your friend. You wrote out directions to the meeting place, but your pal has not shown up. Were your directions unclear? Could your friend be waiting somewhere else?

Route directions must be very specific. The box below shows *direction words* that are often used to explain a route.

above	behind	beneath	beside	east	in front of
inside	left	near	next to	north	outside
over	right	south	straight	under	west

Find and circle two direction words in each item.

1. The ballfield is at the north end of the park, behind the reservoir.

2. To get to the library, go east on Stark Street. Turn left at 49th.

3. The map is buried under the dead oak in front of the red barn.

4. I will meet you just inside the door of the museum's west entrance.

5. Wait under the exit sign next to the theater snack bar.

B

Think about a favorite place to spend your free time. Now write a paragraph explaining how to get there from your home. Circle direction words.

_____

_____

_____

_____

_____

_____

_____

_____

EXPLAINING HOW TO USE IT —34

Think about a time when you bought a new tool, piece of equipment, or appliance. Were the directions easy to follow? Here are some hints for explaining how to use something:

- Keep your purpose in mind. You want to *teach* something.

- Know your audience. Don't use overly technical words.

- Make the instructions easy to follow. Use chronological order and guide the reader with transitional words.

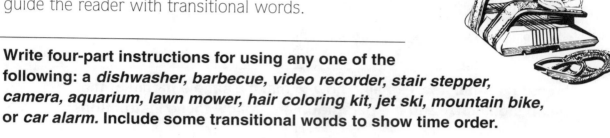

Write four-part instructions for using any one of the following: a *dishwasher, barbecue, video recorder, stair stepper, camera, aquarium, lawn mower, hair coloring kit, jet ski, mountain bike,* or *car alarm.* Include some transitional words to show time order.

1. Define the project. (What is the goal?)

   _____

   _____

   _____

2. Explain preparation and tell how to get started. (Are any other materials needed? What are the first steps in the process?)

   _____

   _____

   _____

3. Identify likely problems.

   _____

   _____

   _____

4. Explain the final steps.

   _____

   _____

   _____

35 Explaining How to Make It

Suppose you are telling someone how to make spaghetti, a dog house, or a computer spreadsheet. Your explanation needs to be very clear. One incorrect step can mean disaster. The following steps will help you write an easy-to-follow paragraph explaining how to make something.

- Write a topic sentence that states the process.
- List the materials needed.
- Write the steps in order.
- Use transitional words such as *before, first, next,* and *finally.*

The paragraph below explains how to make a simple model of the human stomach. Read the paragraph and follow these instructions:

1. **Draw one line under the topic sentence.**

2. **Draw two lines under any materials mentioned.**

3. **Show the order of steps in the process by writing 1, 2, 3, or 4 above the first word in each step.**

4. **Circle any transitional words.**

How to Make a Model of a Stomach

You can make a simple model to show how stomach acids break down food. To begin your model you will need a glass jar, a small piece of cooked beef, and some dilute hydrochloric acid. First, put the beef in the jar. Then carefully add the acid. (Since acids can burn, work carefully!) If any acid spills, wash it off immediately. Next, put the jar in a safe place overnight. On the following day, notice how the beef looks. Compare its appearance before it was soaked in the acid with the way it looks now. The acid in your stomach works on food in much the same way as the acid in your model.

An effective message is short and to the point. A short note need not be written in complete sentences, but it must contain all essential details.

 A

The essential elements of a message are listed below. Identify these elements in the note by writing a letter on the line after each message part. (Hint: You may use some letters more than once.) The first blank has been marked for you.

a. date and time the note was written

b. a greeting telling who the note is for

c. a main point of the message

d. the message writer's name

Tuesday, 9/14, 8:30 P.M. (_a_)

Walt (_____),

    Mr. Arnez phoned—said he'd stop by your office at 9:00 tomorrow morning (_____). You don't need to call him back unless there's a problem (_____). His number: 554-3496 (_____).

                        Sam (_____)

 B

Each message below is missing two important elements. Take another look at the list of elements in Part A. Then write the letters of the missing elements on the lines. The first one has been done as a model.

1. Coach,

    Sorry I missed practice—took my sick dog to the vet. I'll be at tomorrow's practice.

    MISSING ELEMENTS: _a_ , _d_

2. Monday, 5:00 p.m.

    I took three phone calls for you.

    Marge

    MISSING ELEMENTS: _____, _____

3. 5/14, Noon

    The principal's secretary called—said it was urgent that you call back as soon as possible. The number is 249-7796.

    MISSING ELEMENTS: _____, _____

37 WRITING AN ANNOUNCEMENT

Schools, supermarkets, and other public buildings often provide bulletin boards for public notices. People are invited to post announcements there of meetings, dances, and other gatherings.

A

Study the sample bulletin board announcement on the right. Then write a letter to match each definition on the left with an announcement part.

1. _____ when

2. _____ purpose

3. _____ where

4. _____ heading

5. _____ extra information meant to attract people to the gathering

a.→ **GRANT HIGH BOOSTERS CLUB CAR WASH**

b.→ **Proceeds go toward new Pep Band uniforms!**

c.→ **Saturday, June 4—10 A.M. to 4:30 P.M.**

d.→ **Stop and Shop Gas Station
35th and River Road**

e.→ **Hand wash and dry!
Be as proud of your car
as we are of our school!**

B

In the box below, write your own bulletin board notice. Announce a real or imaginary event. Include all the announcement parts described above. Try to give your reader a good reason to attend the event.

_____

_____

_____

_____

_____

_____

_____

_____

Do you need to buy a car? Rent a house? Find a lost pet? Check the classified ads in your newspaper! People buy space in the classified ads section to attract public interest. Remember that ad space is usually sold by the line. Try to reduce your ad copy—and save money—by using abbreviations.

A

Underline each abbreviation. Then write *both* the abbreviation and the word it represents on the lines. The first one has been done for you.

1. 3 <u>BR</u>, 1<u>BA</u> home for rent. <u>Lrg</u> yard, <u>frplc</u>, <u>bsmt</u>. 1 <u>blk</u> from park. $900/<u>mo</u>. No <u>smkg</u>/pets. 617-5942.

   BR=bedroom, BA=bathroom, Lrg=large, frplc=fireplace, bsmt=basement, blk=block, /mo=per month, smkg=smoking

2. 88 Jeep Wrangler, 5spd, low mi, blk, excl cond, $4998, 246-5993.

   _____

   _____

3. Cook needed, FT, for outdr cafe, grill exp req'd. $9.00/hr+benfts. Call Jeff for info, 297-4431.

   _____

   _____

4. Bike, boys Schwinn, 18 sp, like new, orig. $250, sell $175. Lv msg @ 449-7008.

   _____

   _____

B

Do you have something to sell, such as a used skateboard or a baseball card collection? Is there a service you might offer, such as yard care or dog walking? Write a classified ad on the lines below.

_____

_____

_____

_____

WRITING A NEWS ARTICLE

Newspaper articles begin with a *lead paragraph*. This paragraph usually contains one or two sentences that answer the important questions:

●Who?   ●What?   ●When?   ●Where?   ●Why?

A

Read the lead paragraph from a newspaper article. Then answer the questions that follow it.

> While waiting in a Saturday matinee line at the Rogue Theater, Ashland, Oregon, teen Marla McRay, 14, pulled something shiny from a sidewalk trash can. It was a diamond bracelet, worth nearly $10,000.

1. WHO? _____

2. WHAT? _____

3. WHEN? _____

4. WHERE? _____

5. WHY? _____

B

Use the story details to write the lead paragraph for two news articles.

1. DETAILS: • 50 animal rights activists protested against wearing fur

           • Saturday afternoon

           • outside offices of Fordman's Fine Fur Fabricators

           • protesters waved banners and stuffed animals

           • called for a boycott of all products using real fur

_____

_____

_____

_____

_____

_____

2. **DETAILS:**
- 2,000 residents of Crater City without electrical power
- 10 downtown blocks in the dark
- no injuries or major problems reported
- outages began around 11:00 Friday night
- an unusually cold November ice storm
- ice-coated power lines snapped; trees fell
- Crater City Power & Light expected to restore power by Saturday evening

_____
_____
_____
_____
_____
_____
_____
_____

C

Think about recent events in your school. For example, has there been a student government election? Sports victory? Fundraiser? A change in rules or policies? New teacher? Take the role of reporter and write a lead paragraph for a news story. Be sure to answer the questions: *Who? What? When? Where? Why?*

LEAD PARAGRAPH:

_____
_____
_____
_____
_____
_____

WRITING TITLES AND HEADLINES

Titles and *headlines* have two main purposes: (1) They aim to catch a reader's attention, and (2) they suggest what the following story is about.

A

Each group of titles below is intended for the same book. Circle the title you like best. Then tell why you chose that title and what you think the book is about.

1. (a) *Jump Shot Johnny*   (b) *The Basketball Star*   (c) *High School Hero*

   I LIKE THIS TITLE BECAUSE: _____

   THE BOOK SEEMS TO BE ABOUT: _____

2. (a) *Indian Guide*   (b) *Sacajawea: Guide to the Sea*   (c) *Sacajawea*

   I LIKE THIS TITLE BECAUSE: _____

   THE BOOK SEEMS TO BE ABOUT: _____

3. (a) *The Red Twin*   (b) *Mars*   (c) *Another Planet*

   I LIKE THIS TITLE BECAUSE: _____

   THE BOOK SEEMS TO BE ABOUT: _____

B

Notice capitalization in titles and headlines. The first word, the last word, and all important words are capitalized. Little words like *a, an, by, for, from,* or *the* begin with a small letter unless they come first or last. Rewrite each item, capitalizing words correctly.

TITLES:

1. **the black cat** _____

2. **to the lighthouse** _____

3. **the new book of world records** _____

   _____

HEADLINES:

4. **tax hike wins senate approval** _____

   _____

5. **rescued passengers praise teen hero** _____

   _____

C

Make up a title for each of the following selections. Try to catch the reader's interest and suggest the topic.

1. a humorous children's story about the adventures of a pair of panda cubs

   _____

2. an informative article about President Lincoln's assassination

   _____

3. a mystery about the disappearance of a school bus full of students

   _____

4. an essay about your most interesting relative.

   _____

D

Write a headline for each of the following subjects for newspaper articles.

1. A man accused of burglarizing a string of apartment houses is sentenced to 15 years in jail.

   _____

2. The National Education Association selects Ms. Beverly Potts, a science teacher at Ridgeview High, as Teacher of the Year.

   _____

3. Heavy summer rains cause a landslide in the Westover Heights neighborhood. Five homes are destroyed. Two people are injured. The slide blocks Highway 57.

   _____

4. A German shepherd pulls a toddler from a backyard fish pond. The parents, who thought the two-year-old was asleep, credit their pet with saving the child's life.

   _____

Newspapers often hire arts and entertainment critics to review books, films, and television shows. The reviews usually contain the critic's personal opinions backed up by specific examples. Often, the critic uses a scale of some kind to provide an opinion rating.

EXAMPLE: The film *Cool Shade* kept the audience in constant suspense. Nearly every character was a possible murder suspect. At one moment actress Shirley Keen, who convincingly played the greedy widow, seemed to be the killer. Then suspicion suddenly shifted to the evil doctor, played by Rock Branson. For keeping viewers guessing from the first frame to the last, this critic gives *Cool Shade* an *A–*.

A

Imagine that you are an arts and entertainment critic for your local paper. Write a brief movie, television, or book review. Limit the length by focusing on one feature. Use the example above as a model. Be sure to include (a) your opinion about one feature, (b) a specific example to support your opinion, and (c) a rating.

_____

_____

_____

_____

_____

_____

B

Read the following famous quote. Think of a TV show it might apply to. Then write a short criticism of the show.

"Poor reception is about the only way you can improve some television programs." —*Franklin P. Jones*

_____

_____

_____

_____

_____

_____

A Imagine you have invented a useful device that will help its user in daily life. (*Ideas:* an alarm clock that shakes a sleeper awake; a device that stirs food in a pot while the cook moves about the kitchen; a safety candle that blows itself out.) Write a paragraph explaining either how you made your device *or* how to use it. Include a definition of the device in your topic sentence.

_____

_____

_____

_____

_____

_____

_____

B Take the role of a news reporter. Write a headline and a brief article reporting the invention of the device.

_____

_____

_____

_____

_____

_____

_____

C Write a classified ad designed to sell the device.

_____

_____

_____

WRITING TO PERSUADE

FOR HELP WITH GRAMMAR, CAPITALIZATION, PUNCTUATION, OR SPELLING, SEE THE REFERENCE GUIDE ON PAGES 112–128.

UNIT **6**

⟨42⟩ CREATING APPEAL IN AD COPY

The job of an *advertisement* is to sell a product. To win new customers, ad writers appeal to emotion and/or reason. Read the ads below. Notice that the first ad appeals to feelings and emotions while the second appeals to intelligence and reason. Even the names of the products aim specifically for readers' hearts *or* their heads.

AD 1: *Sparkle Yum* toothpaste puts a shine on your teeth and a zesty taste in your mouth. Start your day with *Sparkle Yum*. You'll smile at the world, and the world will smile back!

AD 2: *Denta-Safe* tooth gel dependably whitens teeth while protecting gums. It is tough on bacteria but gentle on enamel. You will find the ICDC (International Council on Dental Care) stamp of approval on every *Denta-Safe* tube.

 A

Study the sample ads above. Write *ad 1* or *ad 2* to answer each question.

1. _____ Which ad more formally writes out the words "you will"?

2. _____ Which ad uses the informal contraction "you'll"?

3. _____ Which ad mentions the "approval of experts"?

4. _____ Which ad emphasizes appearance and good feeling?

5. _____ Which emphasizes safety and dependability?

6. _____ Which ad do *you* find most appealing? Why? _____

_____

_____

_____

B

Read each advertising phrase or product name. On the line write
R or *E* to tell whether it appeals mainly to *reason* or *emotion*. The first
one has been done for you.

1. __R__ higher quality for less cost

2. _____ safe and effective

3. _____ hurry and buy now before you're left out

4. _____ Fiber-Sure Breakfast Bar

5. _____ be the envy of your friends

6. _____ 98% fat free

7. _____ money-back guarantee

8. _____ doctor recommended

9. _____ look like a fashion model

10. _____ contains no harsh chemicals

11. _____ Vita-Sure Nutritional Supplement

12. _____ Zap Soda

13. _____ Spring Breeze Hair Rinse

14. _____ Protein Plus Daily Hair Restorer

15. _____ be the first to own one

C

Imagine yourself as an advertising copywriter. First think of a product,
and then write two ads for it. The first ad should appeal to *emotions* and the
second to *reason*.

1. _____

_____

_____

_____

_____

2. _____

_____

_____

_____

_____

Targeting an Audience

Ad writers consider the age and lifestyles of the *audience* they're trying to reach. What features do you think a cereal ad in a children's magazine would emphasize? What features would a cereal ad in an adult magazine emphasize?

A

Match each product with the age group that would most likely consider buying it. Write C for children, T for teens, or A for adults by each product. Hint: You will name each group more than once.

1. _____ life insurance policy

2. _____ acne cream

3. _____ squirt gun

4. _____ dishwasher

5. _____ action figures

6. _____ rap music CD

7. _____ window shades

8. _____ pogo stick

B

Which product descriptions are likely to interest which consumers? Write a product name in each blank. (You can name real products or use your imagination to invent new product names.)

1. CAR LIKELY TO BE PURCHASED BY A 40-YEAR-OLD: _____

2. CAR LIKELY TO BE PURCHASED BY AN 18-YEAR-OLD: _____

3. A CEREAL THAT WOULD APPEAL TO AN 8-YEAR-OLD: _____

4. A CEREAL THAT WOULD APPEAL TO AN ADULT: _____

5. SKIN CREAM FOR A 16-YEAR-OLD GIRL: _____

6. SKIN CREAM FOR A 16-YEAR-OLD BOY: _____

7. SKIN CREAM FOR A MIDDLE-AGED WOMAN: _____

8. VITAMINS FOR A 6-YEAR-OLD: _____

9. VITAMINS FOR A 25-YEAR-OLD ATHLETE: _____

10. VITAMINS FOR A 60-YEAR-OLD MAN OR WOMAN: _____

Organizing an Argument: Providing Reasons

Suppose you want to convince others to do or believe something. To be persuasive, you must support your suggestion or opinion with at least *three solid reasons*.

A

Each *opinion statement* below is followed by supporting reasons. Three reasons offer good support. Two are off the subject and do not support the argument. Put a check (✓) by each strong supporting reason.

1. Hikers should not go into the wilderness alone.

    _____ a. There should be someone to go for help in case of an injury.

    _____ b. Two hikers are less likely to get lost than a lone hiker.

    _____ c. Hiking can be terrific exercise.

    _____ d. If a problem arises, two heads are always better than one.

    _____ e. Actually, it is probably safer to stay out of the woods.

2. Volunteering can improve a person's life.

    _____ a. Some people are too selfish to help others.

    _____ b. People who help others are happier and healthier themselves.

    _____ c. Volunteers are often rewarded with new friends.

    _____ d. The Red Cross is one of the best volunteer agencies.

    _____ e. Volunteering provides people with new experiences.

B

Complete the following opinion statement and support it with three reasons. Write each reason as a complete sentence.

_____ is the best class this school offers.

1. _____

_____

2. _____

_____

3. _____

_____

Suppose you've already thought of a good reason to support your argument. Your reason will be more convincing if it is supported with an *example* or *fact*.

A

Each item below contains three parts:

1. **an opinion**
2. **a persuasive reason for readers to accept the opinion**
3. **an example or fact that supports the reason**

Circle the opinion. Draw one line under the reason. Draw two lines under the example or fact. Use the first item as a model.

1. (John F. Kennedy was a great man.) As president, he advanced human rights. Kennedy started the Peace Corps, backed civil rights laws, and expanded medical care for the aged.

2. Babysitters should be highly paid. They need a great variety of skills. On my last job I had to cook dinner, entertain three children, fix a broken doll, bandage a cut finger, and break up a fistfight.

3. Teachers should give class credit for travel experiences. Seeing something for yourself can be more educational than reading about it. I had studied the Grand Canyon in science class, but until I visited it, I never realized its true wonders.

4. Wilbur Watson is a jerk. He doesn't care about anyone but himself. Once I saw Wilbur push in front of an elderly lady and grab the last seat on the bus.

B

Write a sentence aimed at persuading readers to eat plenty of a certain food. Follow your opinion sentence with a persuasive reason and at least one example that supports it.

OPINION SENTENCE: _____

_____

REASON: _____

_____

EXAMPLE: _____

_____

DEVELOPING AN ARGUMENT

To present a persuasive written argument you should:

- state your opinion.

- write at least three supporting paragraphs—each with its own topic sentence that presents a persuasive reason.

- develop each paragraph with examples and facts that support the reason.

Plan a persuasive paper. First, think of an opinion that is important to you. (You may use an idea from the box or one of your own.)

• the effect of television watching on grades	• the ideal vacation for teenagers	• the city or country that's the best place to grow up
• the cancellation of your favorite TV show	• the most dangerous sport	• the wisdom of working during the school year
	• the best pet	

Write in complete sentences.

OPINION STATEMENT: _____

_____

REASON 1: _____

_____

EXAMPLE/FACTS: _____

_____

REASON 2: _____

_____

EXAMPLE/FACTS: _____

_____

REASON 3: _____

_____

EXAMPLE/FACTS: _____

_____

— # PUTTING PERSUASION TO WORK

At some time, you may need to present a strong argument for or against something. Be sure to state your opinion clearly and support it with convincing reasons and examples.

A

Present and support your opinion in a letter to the editor of your school or local newspaper.

To the editor of the _____:

_____

_____

_____

_____

_____

_____

_____

_____

Sincerely,

_____

B

Imagine that you are a candidate's campaign manager. Your candidate may be running for mayor of the city or a school or club office. Write a speech persuading voters that your candidate is the best person for the job.

Fellow _____ (students, club members, citizens, etc.):

_____

_____

_____

_____

_____

_____

_____

A Circle the letter of the best answer.

1. When you *persuade*, you: **a.** help someone picture something.
   b. teach a skill.   **c.** get someone to do something or believe something.

2. An *opinion* is: **a.** a fact that can be proven right or wrong.
   b. a belief about something.   **c.** a comparison between two things.

3. To present a strong argument, a writer should back an opinion with at least how many reasons?   **a.** one   **b.** two   **c.** three

4. Which of the following best supports a reason?
   a. sensory details   **b.** repeated opinions   **c.** examples and facts

B Imagine that you are an ad writer. First make up a product, and then complete the following statements.

1. **PRODUCT:** My product is _____.

2. **AUDIENCE:** The people most likely to be interested in my product are _____
   _____.

3. **APPEAL:** Words and phrases such as _____
   _____ will appeal to my audience's emotions.
   Words and phrases such as _____
   _____ will appeal to my audience's reason.

C Do you agree or disagree with the view expressed in this quote?

   "Television has raised writing to a new low."   —*Samuel Goldwyn*

State your opinion about the quote. Then develop a persuasive paragraph with reasons and examples.

_____

_____

_____

_____

_____

_____

_____

WRITING AT SCHOOL
FOR HELP WITH GRAMMAR, CAPITALIZATION, PUNCTUATION, OR SPELLING, SEE THE REFERENCE GUIDE ON PAGES 112–128.

UNIT

7

48 — ANSWERING ESSAY QUESTIONS

Some test questions ask students to answer with a brief essay of one or more paragraphs. When faced with an essay question, remember the basic guidelines of paragraph writing plus these hints.

- In your topic sentence rewrite the question as a statement. The topic sentence should also show how the answer will develop.

  EXAMPLE ASSIGNMENT: *Describe three characteristics of the koala bear.*

  TOPIC SENTENCE: *Three special features make the koala bear an unusual animal.*

- Write only information that answers the question.

- Look for instruction words, such as *summarize* (present main points), *describe* (create a word picture), *explain* (clarify with details), *compare* (tell similarities and differences), or *discuss* (give good and bad points, share your opinion). Make sure you do exactly what is asked.

- Watch for numbers. For example, does the question ask you to give *three* reasons or discuss *two* points?

A

Read the boldfaced essay assignments. Then do the following for each: (a) *Circle* the key instruction word. (b) Put a *box* around any numbers. (c) Write a sentence that restates the question as a statement. Use the first item as a model.

1. (Describe) three ways the invention of the telephone changed people's lives.

   The invention of the telephone changed the daily lives of Americans in three important ways.

2. **Describe two gods worshipped by the ancient Greeks.**

   _____

3. **Describe four stages in the life cycle of a butterfly.**

   _____

4. **Explain the workings of the human ear.**

   _____

B

Write essay answers for these questions.

1. Describe three features of your community's public transportation system. (Your answer should create a mental picture of the system.)

_____

_____

_____

_____

_____

2. Discuss your community's public transportation system. (Your answer should identify good and bad points and give your opinion.)

_____

_____

_____

_____

_____

_____

C

Write _yes_ or _no_ to evaluate the essay answers you wrote in Part B.

_____ I restated the question in both topic sentences.

_____ I noticed the word _three_ in question 1, and I described three features of the system.

_____ In question 1, I provided descriptive details of three features.

_____ In question 2, I presented my opinions of the good and bad points of the system.

_____ I wrote a well-developed paragraph with a topic sentence, a body of supporting details, and a concluding sentence.

D

If you answered _no_ to any of the items above, go back to Part B and revise your answer.

WRITING A BOOK REPORT

There are many ways to report on a book. Notice how the following book report shows your understanding of the story elements.

A

Read the sample report below. Then answer the questions.

TITLE: Company Secret   **AUTHOR:** Roger Overnout

SETTING: The story takes place in Bridgeton, a town in rural Oklahoma. The time is not directly stated but appears to be the present.

MAIN CHARACTERS: Kelly Scout, Tim Tenasco, Bosco Bridges, Scoop Reed

CHARACTER SKETCH: Kelly Scout is a 16-year-old high school student. She lives with her father, owner of Bridgeton's general store. Kelly is withdrawn and studious. Her father has taught her that young girls should know their place—and that place is at home! A special friendship with Tim Tenasco brings Kelly out of her shell.

PLOT:

   Conflict/Problem: Kelly learns a deadly secret about how Bridgeco, the local chemical factory, handles hazardous waste. But how can she prove accusations against its powerful owner, Bosco Bridges?

   Main Incident: Kelly is trapped in a pit at the Bridgeco dump. She is nearly buried alive when a steam shovel begins to fill the pit with waste! Luckily, Tim arrives in time to save her.

   Resolution of Conflict: Kelly and Tim find proof of Bosco Bridges' crimes on his computer hard drive. They take their evidence to the local newspaper. The town is saved from deadly contamination.

RECOMMENDATION: The story was packed with suspense since Kelly was often in danger. I related to Kelly's shyness. I liked seeing how she built courage and self-confidence. I recommend this book to readers who like suspense, are interested in science and ecology, and also enjoy a bit of romance.

---

1. Who wrote *Company Secret*? _____

2. When and where did the story take place? _____

3. Who are the heroes of this story? _____

4. Who is the villain? _____

5. Write two adjectives that describe Kelly Scout. _____

6. What was one reason the reader liked the book? _____

_____

B

Fill out this form to report on a book you have read. As a model, use the example book report on page 74.

TITLE: _____   AUTHOR: _____

SETTING (TIME AND PLACE OF THE STORY): _____

_____

MAIN CHARACTERS: _____

CHARACTER SKETCH: _____

_____

_____

_____

_____

PLOT:

   CONFLICT: _____

_____

_____

   MAIN INCIDENT: _____

_____

_____

_____

   RESOLUTION OF CONFLICT: _____

_____

_____

RECOMMENDATION: _____

_____

_____

_____

_____

You may sometimes get a chance to use your imagination in book reporting.

Read the ideas below and select *one*. Then use that method to report on the book you wrote about on page 75.

- Write a letter of appreciation to the author.

- Write a different ending to the story.

- Imagine you're a character in the book. Write a letter to another character discussing a story incident.

- Compare this book to one that has a similar theme, topic, character, or setting.

- Write a letter to your local library board. Try to persuade them to add this book to their collection.

- Create a cartoon strip showing a main incident in the book.

_____

_____

_____

_____

_____

_____

_____

_____

_____

_____

_____

_____

_____

_____

_____

_____

CHOOSING A TOPIC FOR A SHORT RESEARCH PAPER

Writing a research paper can seem like a big job. If you approach it step-by-step, however, the task becomes much easier. Step one is *choosing a topic*.

 A

Writing a paper can be more enjoyable if you choose a topic you like. The research will give you a chance to learn more about a topic that interests you. Next to each subject listed below, write a topic you would enjoy learning more about.

1. A HISTORICAL EVENT: _____

2. A FAMOUS PERSON: _____

3. A HOBBY: _____

4. AN INVENTION OR A TECHNOLOGICAL DEVELOPMENT: _____

5. A HEALTH ISSUE: _____

 B

Make sure your topic is the right size. If you research a topic that is too broad, it will be difficult to sort through enough information to cover the whole topic. If you select a topic that is too narrow or little known, however, you may find too little information. Read each group of ideas listed below. Then circle the letter of the topic that seems just the right size for a three-page research paper.

1. **a.** basketball

    b. the Utah Jazz

    c. the Hamilton High Hawks

2. **a.** the praying mantis

    b. insects

    c. my ant farm

3. **a.** how to do a magic trick

    b. magic

    c. world famous magicians

4. **a.** my uncle, Ensign Ben Cole

    b. the Navy

    c. the history of navy submarines

5. **a.** automobiles

    b. Henry Ford and the Model T

    c. our new Ford minivan

52 — FINDING SOURCES AND TAKING NOTES

Once you have a topic, you are ready to begin your research. Books and periodicals are a good place to start. Magazines and newspapers can often provide much of the information you need. You might also use information from a television program, or you could interview an expert.

A

Read the terms on the left. You are likely to use these resources in your library research. Write a letter to match each term with its description.

1. _____ **card or computer catalog**

2. _____ **periodicals**

3. _____ **Readers' Guide**

4. _____ **encyclopedia**

5. _____ **almanac**

6. _____ **atlas**

7. _____ **Current Biography**

a. publications such as newspapers or magazines that are published at regular intervals

b. a book of maps and facts about places

c. a multi-volume reference source containing alphabetized entries on almost every subject

d. an alphabetized source of information for every book in the library, listed according to subject, title, or author

e. a set of books with information about famous people; entries are listed alphabetically

f. a book of facts, statistics, and other information for current and past years

g. volumes listing articles from major magazines

B

List three sources you could check to find information on each topic.

1. Tiger Woods

_____

_____

_____

2. heart transplants

_____

_____

_____

Writers often make research notes on index cards. The cards can be easily organized according to subtopics.

Read the article. Underline ideas you would include in notes for a paper on Amelia Earhart.

Amelia Earhart's fame began in 1928 when she became the first woman to cross the Atlantic in an airplane. At that time, she was a passenger. In 1932 she made piloting history as the first woman to fly across the Atlantic alone. In 1935, Earhart was in the headlines again. She was the first pilot—man or woman—to solo across the Pacific.

Amelia Earhart was born in Kansas in 1898. When she was 10, she went to the Iowa State Fair and saw her first airplane. That day she fell in love with flying. Thirteen years later she began taking flying lessons. Earhart spent some time in medical school and two years as a social worker. Eventually, however, she devoted most of her life to flying.

In 1937, Amelia Earhart was ready to chase her biggest dream. She would fly around the world! The trip was too difficult to undertake alone, so Fred Noonan went along as navigator. The pair flew a plane called the *Electra* from California to Florida, then on to South America, Africa, India, and Southeast Asia. Then, in a stretch of sky over the Pacific Ocean, the *Electra* disappeared. No trace of the plane, Amelia Earhart, or Fred Noonan was ever found.

B

Each of the note cards shown below has been headed with a subtopic. Write two ideas from the article on each card.

AMELIA EARHART'S EARLY LIFE

1. _____
_____
_____
2. _____
_____
_____

EARHART'S HISTORIC FLIGHTS

1. _____
_____
_____
2. _____
_____
_____

EARHART'S LAST FLIGHT

1. _____
_____
_____
2. _____
_____
_____

— **GIVING CREDIT TO SOURCES**

As a researcher, you will find your information in various sources. It is important to give credit to each source you use.

A

When you directly quote an author, put the words in quotation marks and identify the *source*. Read the passages below. Draw two lines under each direct quotation. Circle its source.

1. In *Amelia's Sky*, author Clifton Hughes quotes Earhart as saying, "I have often said that the lure of flying is the lure of beauty."

2. According to R. J. Rex's biography, *Lost*, Amelia Earhart left a letter marked "To be opened in case of death." The letter read: "Hooray for the last grand adventure! I wish I had won. . . ."

B

Sources are always listed in a *bibliography* at the end of a research paper. Study the sample entries below. Then write *T* or *F* to tell whether each statement about bibliographies is *true* or *false*.

> **Earhart, Amelia.** Learning World Encyclopedia, Vol. 2. Chicago: New School Publications, 1996, pp. 109–110.
>
> **Hughes, Clifton.** Amelia's Sky. New York: Smith and Lake, Inc., 1972.
>
> **Kellogg, Nan.** "Search for Electra," Aviation Monthly, May '93, Vol. 4, p. 15.
>
> **Long, Anna.** Women of the Century. Seattle: Wilson Brent Co., 1998.
>
> **Rex, R. J.** Strange Disappearances. Boston: Waterton Publishing, 1988.

1. _____ Bibliographic entries are arranged in alphabetical order.

2. _____ If an entry is more than one line, the first line is indented.

3. _____ The title of a book is underlined.

4. _____ The title of a magazine article is underlined.

5. _____ In an encyclopedia entry, the name of the encyclopedia appears first.

6. _____ The author's last name begins a book entry.

UNIT REVIEW

A Circle the letter of the item that best completes each sentence.

1. In the topic sentence of an answer to an essay question, you should: **a.** recopy the question word for word. **b.** rewrite the question as a statement. **c.** give an opinion about the question.

2. In an essay question, the instruction word "discuss" tells the writer to: **a.** compare the topic with something similar. **b.** tell the answer out loud. **c.** present good and bad points and opinions.

3. An answer to an essay question should be written in: **a.** complete sentences. **b.** paragraph form. **c.** both a and b.

4. It is a good idea to take research notes on: **a.** index cards. **b.** paper towels. **c.** computer disks.

5. A bibliography is a: **a.** book of maps. **b.** list of sources. **c.** list of all the books in a library.

B Choose one of the following essay questions and write an answer.

1. Explain this quote by Dorothy Parker: *"This is not a novel to be tossed aside lightly. It should be thrown with great force."*

2. Summarize four important steps in writing a research paper.

3. Discuss the effect of Amelia Earhart's achievements on the role of women in America. (Refer to information on pages 79 and 80.)

_____

_____

_____

_____

_____

_____

_____

BUSINESS WRITING

UNIT **8**

FOR HELP WITH GRAMMAR, CAPITALIZATION, PUNCTUATION, OR SPELLING, SEE THE REFERENCE GUIDE ON PAGES 112–128.

55 — WRITING A BUSINESS LETTER

A *business letter* has six parts. Read the business letter below. Notice that the writer is asking for information.

1. HEADING

3659 N. Wilson Avenue
Bells Harbor, MA 07660
May 25, 1999

2. INSIDE ADDRESS

Bigfoot Shoe Shop
402 N.W. Irving Street
Clark City, MD 27005

3. GREETING

Dear Customer Service Director:

4. BODY

I am writing to request your free catalog. A radio advertisement called my attention to your store. I understand you specialize in large shoe sizes. Since I wear a size 16 Wide, I am most interested in what you have to offer. Along with your product catalog, I would like information about your mail order procedures and exchange policies.

Please send the catalog to the address above. I am pleased to learn of your specialty store. I hope that your shop will be the answer to my footwear needs.

5. CLOSING

Sincerely,

6. SIGNATURE

Matt Delaney
Matt Delaney

A

Read the elements of a business letter listed on the left. Write a letter to match each element with its location.

1. _____ name and address of business

2. _____ :

3. _____ ,

4. _____ writer's address

5. _____ main message

6. _____ writer's handwritten name

a. punctuation after greeting

b. punctuation after closing

c. within the body

d. within the heading

e. within the inside address

f. signature

B

Reread the letter on page 82. Then read the statements about that letter. Write T or F to tell whether each statement is true or false.

1. _____ The first sentence in Matt's letter clearly states his reason for writing.

2. _____ Matt failed to include his zip code in his home address.

3. _____ Matt didn't know the name of the person he was writing to.

4. _____ Matt won't visit shoe stores because the clerks are rude.

5. _____ Matt wants to know if he can return a pair of shoes he doesn't like.

56 — WRITING A LETTER OF COMPLAINT

Have you ever been disappointed in a product's performance or a company's service? That may have been a good time to write a *letter of complaint*. To get results, however, a letter should do more than just complain. It should:

- *Clearly state the specific problem.* Don't merely complain that the service was lousy. Specify, for example, that workers did not arrive at the promised time and that the job was never completed.

- *Suggest a reasonable solution.* Tell how long you expect to wait for action. For example, ask that workers return within the week or that the company reduce your bill.

A

Think of three disappointing services or products that you have purchased in the past. Describe each specific problem.

1. _____

2. _____

3. _____

B

Focus on *one* of the problems listed above. How did you handle it? How do you *wish* it had been resolved? On the lines below, tell what actually happened. If the result was less than satisfactory, describe a better solution.

_____

_____

_____

_____

_____

_____

_____

C

Read the following letter of complaint. How could it be improved?

444 N. Alberta Street
Littleburg, PA 19910

Sunny's Stereo World
516 Borderline Boulevard
Littleburg, PA 19432

Hey Dudes!

I recently bought a pair of Boomburg stereo speakers at your store. What junk! Not only did they *not* blast my neighbors' ears off as you promised, but they're falling apart! How can you sell such garbage!

Your Angry Ex-customer,

Rocky Ridges

Rewrite Rocky's letter in a way that is more likely to get results. Be specific about the problem, and politely suggest a reasonable way to remedy the situation. (Invent any information you like.)

_____

_____

_____

_____

_____

_____

_____

_____

_____

_____

_____

_____

_____

Writing a letter is often the first step in applying for a job. You might write to answer a job ad, approach an employer, or follow up on an interview. Use the standard business letter format. The checklist below explains what to include in the body of your letter.

- [ ] **the name of the position that interests you**
- [ ] **your educational background and availability**
- [ ] **a short summary of your experience and qualifications**
- [ ] **a request for an interview**

A

Think of a job you'd enjoy. Then write a letter of application. You may make up information if you wish.

_____

_____

_____

_____

_____

_____

_____

_____

_____

_____

_____

_____

_____

_____

_____

_____

B

Compare your letter to the checklist at the top of the page. Put a check (✓) by each item you included in your letter.

A résumé is a summary of a job-seeker's education, experience, and skills. It gives an employer an overview of a job applicant's background.

Jed Washington
1932 Monroe Street
Bozeman, MT 59715
Phone: (412) 777-1392
e-mail: jwash@telex.com

Education   Central High School, Bozeman, Montana. Graduated June 1997.

Work Experience

6/96–present   *Construction assistant.* Franz Contractors, P.O. Box 917, Bozeman, Montana, 59715. Assisted in home framing and finish work. Received training in carpentry, basic electrical wiring, and plumbing.

6/95–9/95   *Playground supervisor.* Bozeman Public Parks Department, 413 Main St., Bozeman, Montana, 59716. Maintained park equipment and facilities; supervised usage.

5/94–5/95   *Yard maintenance.* Provided residential lawn and garden care. Duties included mowing, trimming, and fertilizing. Scheduled and billed clients; kept records.

Community Activities

9/96–present   Bozeman Big Brothers program—mentor and tutor for boys, ages 6–10.

6/94–9/94   Volunteer host for Bozeman Public Parks. Led weekend tours of city gardens.

Skills   Basic landscaping, carpentry, electrical, and plumbing. Hold "Master Gardener" certificate from Green's Nursery.

References   Available upon request.

58

Circle a letter to complete each sentence. If you need help, look back at the résumé on page 87.

1. A *résumé* lists experience beginning with **a.** your most recent experience. **b.** your first experience. **c.** your most impressive experience.

2. The fact that a job applicant can type 50 wpm would go under the résumé heading **a.** *Community Activities.* **b.** *Skills.* **c.** *Education.*

3. Your *references* are **a.** types of jobs you'd like to have. **b.** places you have lived. **c.** people who can give information about you.

4. Unpaid work for a charity group should **a.** appear under *Education.* **b.** not be listed on a résumé. **c.** appear under *Community Activities.*

B

A résumé may or may not list references. Think of two or three former employers, volunteer supervisors, coaches, teachers, or co-workers you could use as references. (In a real résumé, you must get their permission before listing their names.) Now list the names, positions, and addresses of two references. Follow the labeled model below.

Model:	**1. NAME**	Ms. Beth Amado
	2. POSITION	Red Cross Volunteer Coordinator
	3. ADDRESS	1312 Market Street
		Seattle, WA 98119

1. _____   2. _____

_____   _____

_____   _____

_____   _____

C

Write a résumé for yourself or an imaginary job applicant. As a guide, use the model on page 87.

COMPLETING A JOB APPLICATION

When you apply for a job, you'll probably fill out an application. Be prepared by bringing a list of information such as addresses and dates. The following checklist gives some job application hints.

- [ ] **Read through the whole application before filling it out.**
- [ ] **Fill in every item or write *NA*, which stands for *not applicable*.**
- [ ] **Spell, capitalize, and punctuate carefully.**
- [ ] **Print neatly.**
- [ ] **Where space is limited, write only recent, relevant information.**
- [ ] **Include zip codes and area codes.**

A

Think about the impression you want to create with your completed job application. Then circle the word that you think makes each statement true.

1. It would be a (good / bad) idea to fill out a job application in sparkling gold ink.

2. If you forget the dates you held former jobs, it (is / is not) all right to make them up.

3. If you're applying for a laborer's job, accurate spelling (does / does not) apply.

4. The employer will be (turned off / impressed) if you write "none of your business" next to some questions.

5. Job applications (do / do not) require you to list your hobbies and favorite foods.

6. "If I don't get this job I'll starve" is (a clever / an inappropriate) line to add to a job application.

B

Think of a job you'd like and write it below. Then fill out the following form to apply for that job. When you complete the application, use the checklist on page 90 to evaluate your work.

POSITION: _____

Job Application
XYZ COMPANY

NAME: First/Initial/Last	Telephone No.:

ADDRESS: Number and Street	Apt. #:

City/State/Zip	

Telephone No.:	Social Security No.:	Date Available for Work:

PREVIOUS JOBS (paid and volunteer)

Employer:	Address:

Supervisor/Contact:	Telephone No.:

Position Held:	Dates of Employment:	Reason for Leaving:

Employer:	Address:

Supervisor/Contact:	Telephone No.:

Position Held:	Dates of Employment:	Reason for Leaving:

Last year of education completed:

School:	Address:	Year Completed:

Explain why you qualify for this position.

A Complete each statement by filling in the blanks.

1. Three reasons for writing a business letter are to _____

    _____, _____,

    and _____.

2. Three writing tasks you would likely perform during the job hunting

    process are _____, _____

    _____, and _____.

3. When you apply for a job, you should take along information such as

    _____ and _____.

B Write **Y** by items that *would* be listed on a résumé and **N** by those
items that would *not* be listed.

1. _____ education

2. _____ work experience

3. _____ phone number

4. _____ salary requirements

5. _____ community activities

6. _____ height and weight

7. _____ skills

8. _____ paragraph telling why
you want the job

9. _____ address

10. _____ emergency contacts

C Revise and improve the following letter of application. Use your imagination to provide missing information.

Dear Person in Charge of Hiring for Wilson Brothers Home Builders,

I would like a job on your construction crew. I work out, am very strong, and really need the muney. I culd be a carpenter's helper because I've helped my Uncle Ted build bookcases. I could start work this sumer. How does $10.00 an hour sound? I would need to make at least that much, because, as Samuel Johnson once said, "No man loves labor for itself!" Pleese call me.

From, Bill LaVoit, 3192 N.W. Aspen Dr., Welcometon, TX 75132

_____

_____

_____

_____

_____

_____

_____

_____

_____

_____

_____

_____

_____

_____

_____

_____

SOCIAL WRITING

FOR HELP WITH GRAMMAR, CAPITALIZATION, PUNCTUATION, OR SPELLING, SEE THE REFERENCE GUIDE ON PAGES 112–128.

UNIT
9

60 — ANALYZING A FRIENDLY LETTER

A *friendly letter* is less formal than a business letter. It does, however, have a proper format. Notice the five parts of the example letter below.

1. HEADING
(your address
and the date)

284 North Post Road
Muckiwama, ID 83501
June 14, 1999

2. GREETING

Dear Ralph,

3. BODY

It is day six for me here at Camp Muckiwama. I think I'm going to like being a counselor. The 8-year-olds in my cabin sure keep me busy.

I must tell you about one boy in particular. His name is Buddy Bentley. Ralph, he reminds me so much of us when we were kids! He's always getting into trouble. Last night he put lizards in all the bunks. I knew I had to discipline him, but it was hard to keep from laughing!

Do you like your bike messenger job? You must get your daily dose of excitement riding in the downtown traffic! Be careful! How is the rest of the gang back home? Don't forget about me out here in the wilderness. Remind everyone to drop me a note. Until later . . . "So long, Scout." (That's how Muckiwama campers sign off!)

4. CLOSING

Your pal,

5. SIGNATURE

Ben

A

Reread the sample letter from Ben at Camp Muckiwama. Copy a sentence from the letter that does each of the following:

1. tells how Ben is and how he is feeling

_____

2. tells something of interest that has happened

_____

3. shows Ben's interest in Ralph's life

_____

4. invites Ralph to answer the letter

_____

B

Each pair of items below shows two versions of the same element of a friendly letter. First write the name of the element. Then circle the correctly written item. The first one has been done for you.

1. LETTER PART(S): _____*salutation*_____

   (a. Dear Annie,)   b. Dear Annie:

2. LETTER PART(S): _____

   a. yours truly! Bob   b. Yours truly,
                                Bob

3. LETTER PART(S): _____

   a. May 5 1999   b. 222 West 19th Street
      222 West 19th Street   Zipville, VT 05641
      Zipville VT 05641   May 5, 1999

4. LETTER PART(S): _____

   a. Sincerely,   b. Sincerely:
      Bob   *Mr. Walter J. Smith, Jr.*
                                Mr. Walter J. Smith, Jr.

WRITING A FRIENDLY LETTER

A

Write a letter to a friend who has moved away. Tell about what your friends have been up to and what's going on at school. Add the types of information included in the example letter on page 94. You may write about real events or make up details.

_____

_____

_____

_____

_____

_____

_____

_____

_____

_____

_____

_____

_____

_____

_____

_____

_____

_____

B

Specific details and examples add interest to letters. Avoid overused sayings such as "Having a wonderful time . . ." or "Wish you were here. . . ." On the lines below, write two or three sentences that could replace the worn-out sayings with specific news and details. The first one has been done for you.

"Everyone misses you . . ."

Just the other day Josh said that our fishing trips aren't as much fun since you moved away. And science class isn't nearly as exciting without your crazy experiments!

"Having a wonderful time . . ."

_____

_____

_____

_____

"Wish you were here . . ."

_____

_____

_____

_____

C

Read the sentences about friendly letters. Write *T* or *F* to show whether each statement is *true* or *false*.

1. _____ It is rude to mention any problems or upsetting news in a friendly letter.

2. _____ A friendly letter always includes the complete address of the person you are writing to.

3. _____ A friendly letter must be at least five paragraphs in length.

4. _____ A friendly letter is not complete without a greeting and a closing.

LETTERS OF APOLOGY AND CONDOLENCE

It can be hard to write a letter saying you are sorry. Perhaps, however, you need to apologize for something you did that was hurtful or thoughtless. Or perhaps you want to express your sympathy to someone whose friend or relative has died.

A

When a friend's brother dies, this writer offers sympathy to the parents. First, read the letter. Then read the suggestions listed below and put a check (✓) by each idea the letter includes.

1229 Braxton Avenue
Scottsburg, NC 28804
July 30, 1999

Dear Mr. and Mrs. Martin,

I was sorry to hear about your son Steven's death. He was a generous person and never too busy to spend time with the younger guys. We all looked up to him and will miss him a lot.

My thoughts are with you and Steven's brothers and sisters. The next time I'm in the neighborhood, I'll drop by to say hello.

With sympathy,

Sam Gomez

The letter includes:

1. _____ an expression of sorrow

2. _____ a compliment about the person who died

3. _____ respects to other family members

4. _____ cheerful comments on another topic

5. _____ an offer of help

6. _____ news of what the writer has been doing

B

Think about a time you needed to make an apology. Perhaps you missed an important event, hurt someone's feelings, or neglected a duty. Write a note of apology in the form of a friendly letter. The situation you write about may be real or imaginary.

C

Write a sympathy note to a friend whose grandmother has died.

(63) INVITATIONS AND THANK YOU NOTES

One reason for writing a friendly letter is to offer an invitation. Here is the basic information that should be included in an invitation:

☐ **the name of the event**

☐ **the exact time and date**

☐ **place where the event will be held**

☐ **whether or not guests should bring anything**

☐ **request for a response, if you'd like one (The letters RSVP mean "please answer.")**

A

Write a letter inviting someone to a real or an imaginary event. (*Ideas:* sports event, party, concert, music recital, special ceremony, reunion.) Follow the format of a friendly letter.

_____

_____

_____

_____

_____

_____

_____

_____

_____

_____

_____

_____

_____

B

Compare your letter to the checklist just above it. Check off each item that appears in your invitation.

C

Think about a time when someone gave you a gift or did something special for you. Write that person a thank you note. In the first sentence, tell what you are grateful for. Go on to describe at least two specific details you appreciated.

_____

_____

_____

_____

_____

_____

_____

_____

_____

_____

_____

_____

D

Read the sentences about invitations and thank you notes.
Write *T* or *F* to show whether each statement is *true* or *false*.

1. _____ Unless the invitation is for a special occasion, you don't have to tell people what to wear.

2. _____ All invitations tell people what time to go home.

3. _____ Thank you notes are sent only to casual acquaintances, not family members.

4. _____ The letters *RSVP* are always added to a thank you note.

A Choose one of the following situations. Write a friendly letter to suit the occasion. Use your imagination.

- A summer job has taken you far away, and you're writing home.

- Your teacher's husband or wife has died, and you are writing a sympathy note.

- You are inviting someone to celebrate your graduation from clown college.

- You are thanking a grandparent for a surprise gift.

_____

_____

_____

_____

_____

_____

_____

_____

_____

_____

_____

_____

_____

_____

_____

_____

B Review the letter you wrote in Part A. Label these letter parts:

1. *heading*   2. *greeting*   3. *body*   4. *closing*   5. *signature*

ARTFUL WRITING

FOR HELP WITH GRAMMAR, CAPITALIZATION, PUNCTUATION, OR SPELLING, SEE THE REFERENCE GUIDE ON PAGES 112–128.

UNIT
10

64 PLANNING A STORY

A *story* tells about something that happened. While the events can be made up or true, all stories have the same basic elements. It is important to think through each element before you write a story.

Outline a story. It can be a story you've already read or a story you would like to write. Make a story map by writing ideas for each story element.

Conflict: Write a sentence stating the problem or struggle the story revolves around.

_____

_____

Setting: Tell where and when the story takes place.

_____

_____

Characters: List the people involved in resolving the conflict.

_____

_____

Point of View: Will the story be told by a character who is part of the action or by an outside narrator?

_____

Main Events: Describe happenings that lead to resolving the conflict.

_____

_____

_____

Resolution: Write a sentence explaining the outcome of the struggle or the solution to the problem.

_____

_____

Without a *conflict*, there is no story.

A

Decide whether each of the following passages contains a conflict or not. Write *Conflict* or *No Conflict* after each passage.

1.   Laura and her 14-year-old daughter Lulu felt lucky. They were near the front of a long line of people waiting to see the hit movie *Clash of the Comets*. Laura looked toward the ticket booth. Then she turned back to Lulu. "It's a good thing we bought tickets ahead of time," she said. "The cashier is saying this show is sold out." _____

2.   Laura and her 14-year-old daughter Lulu felt lucky. They were near the front of a long line of people waiting to see the hit movie *Clash of the Comets*. Laura looked toward the ticket booth. She was anxious for the line to get moving. Then she turned back to talk to Lulu. But her daughter was gone. In her place stood a stranger— a girl with dark hair and a vacant stare.
     "What's the matter, Mom?" the stranger asked. _____

B

Think of a situation that contains conflict. It can be a real experience or an imagined one. Write a story opener that clearly presents a problem or struggle. As a model, use the passage from Part A that contains conflict.

_____

_____

_____

_____

_____

_____

_____

_____

_____

Characters are the imaginary people involved in a story's conflict. Writers want their readers to care about their characters. They use descriptive details and *dialogue* (conversation) to bring their characters to life.

Read the story opener. Answer the questions that follow.

It was midnight when Joe pulled his Chevy pickup into the driveway. Working overtime was tough, but Joe was a hard-working kind of guy. Although he was exhausted, he smiled when he looked at his darkened house. He thought of his wife and kids safely sleeping inside.

Joe took a deep breath of night air and started to cough. Suddenly, he noticed a smoky smell. He saw a dense haze around the street light. Now Joe was wide awake. Smoke was drifting out the window of his neighbor's house! Flames were shooting from the roof. Without a thought for his own safety, Joe dashed toward the burning house.

"Fire!" Joe yelled as he ran. "Someone wake up! Call 911!"

"Joe!" his wife Anna screamed from their window. "Don't go in! It's not safe!"

"But they have *children*!" Joe cried. "I must save the children!"

1. Do you *like* or *dislike* Joe? _____

2. What good quality does the author describe Joe as having? _____

   _____

3. What is one thing Joe does that makes you feel as you do about him?

   _____

4. Copy a line of dialogue that makes you have feelings for Joe. _____

   _____

   _____

66

Look back at your story map and the opener you wrote on page 104. Try to visualize your characters. If you can "see them in your mind's eye" the chances are your readers will be able to see them, too.

B

Write descriptions of two characters. What do they look like? Tell something about their personalities as well.

FIRST CHARACTER: _____

_____

_____

_____

SECOND CHARACTER: _____

_____

_____

_____

C

Reread the characters' dialogue on page 105. Then think about your own characters and what they might say. On the lines below, write some dialogue for your characters that will create an emotional response in your reader.

_____

_____

_____

_____

_____

_____

_____

_____

_____

_____

_____

Setting describes the time and place a story happens. These elements should be made clear early in the story. The writer can directly state the setting or suggest it through a series of clues.

⟨A⟩

Reread the story opener on page 105. Then answer the questions.

1. At what time of day does the story take place? _____
   How do you know? _____

2. Is the story set in the present day, in a time long past, or far into the
   future? _____ How do you know? _____
   _____

3. In what specific place does the story unfold? _____
   _____

4. Does Joe lives in the United States, a foreign country, a city, or a farm?
   _____ What clues suggest this? _____
   _____

⟨B⟩

The setting can create a *mood*, or feeling. Notice that placing the action at darkest midnight rather than in daylight sets up a mood. Rewrite the story opener below. Add setting details to create either a mood of danger and mystery or of bright, happy times.

   I left the building by the back door. I walked toward the parking lot.
When I reached my car, I saw that something was different. _____
_____
_____
_____
_____
_____
_____

PLOT: CONFLICT, CLIMAX, AND RESOLUTION

A story's *plot* is the chain of events that leads to the outcome. Ask yourself: "What happens to resolve the conflict of this story?"

A

Think about the character, Joe, whom you met on page 105. The story plot begins as Joe faces a problem: *His neighbor's house is on fire—but he may risk his own life if he tries to help.* Think about what will happen next. How will the problem be solved? Use your imagination to come up with events that could complete the plot. The last event you list should be the *climax*—the high point of the story.

EVENTS LEADING TO RESOLUTION: _____

_____

_____

CLIMAX: _____

RESOLUTION: _____

_____

B

Coming up with a believable solution can take imagination! Read the following problems. For each problem, fill in events, a climax, and a resolution.

1. David sees a long hunting knife in his best friend Seth's school backpack. He knows that Seth has a terrible temper.

EVENTS LEADING TO RESOLUTION: _____

_____

_____

_____

_____

CLIMAX: _____

_____

RESOLUTION: _____

_____

_____

2. The warning sirens are blasting. Everyone must evacuate the town before the hurricane hits. But Selina can't find her grandmother.

EVENTS LEADING TO RESOLUTION: _____

_____

_____

_____

_____

_____

CLIMAX: _____

_____

RESOLUTION: _____

_____

_____

3. The railroad bridge near Karen's home is washed out. The phone lines are down. Someone must warn the station master to stop the midnight express before it gets to the bridge! Karen jumps in her car—but it won't start.

EVENTS LEADING TO RESOLUTION: _____

_____

_____

_____

_____

_____

CLIMAX: _____

_____

RESOLUTION: _____

_____

_____

A Read this story opener. Then complete the activities listed below it.

Kevin T. McKay was 12 years old. His friends said the *T.* in his name stood for *trouble*, but, actually, it stood for Thomas. One Saturday morning Kevin T. was bored. As he entered the kitchen, his eyes darted about, looking for something to do. He spied a yellow envelope on the counter and saw that it was addressed to his mother. When he saw the words "Win $1,000," however, Kevin decided to read on! The letter inside announced a big cooking contest. It offered a cash prize for a healthful recipe using unusual ingredients.

"What luck!" Kevin said aloud. He had just finished reading an article about the high protein content of certain edible insects.

1. Describe the setting. _____

_____

2. Write the name of the main character. _____

3. Explain how you feel about the main character and why. _____

_____

_____

_____

4. Imagine a problem that is likely to develop. _____

_____

_____

5. Suggest a possible outcome. _____

_____

_____

_____

B Rewrite the following sentences to convey a mysterious mood.

1. The door opened. _____

2. The house was big. _____

3. He stood on the beach. _____

C Plan an exciting story of your own. Make a story map on the lines below.

Conflict: _____

_____

_____

Setting: _____

_____

Characters: _____

_____

_____

Point of View: _____

_____

Main Events: _____

_____

_____

_____

_____

_____

Resolution: _____

_____

_____

_____

GRAMMAR AND USAGE REFERENCE GUIDE

═ SENTENCES ═

❶ The Sentence: A Complete Thought

A sentence is a language unit that contains a subject and a predicate and expresses a complete thought. A written sentence begins with a capital letter and ends with a period, a question mark, or an exclamation point.

I have two dozen CD's in my collection.
How many CD's do you have?
Listen to this one!

Some complete sentences have only one word. In sentences such as these, the subject is understood to be *you*.

Stop. Help!

❷ Subjects and Predicates

The two main parts of a sentence are the subject and the predicate. The subject names what the sentence is about. It may be a word, a phrase, or a clause.

Dogs are the most loyal pets.
Losing a dog is very sad.

The predicate is the part of the sentence that tells something about the subject. It includes the verb as well as all other words that are not part of the subject.

My brother *is the boy with red hair.*
Is your sister *meeting us in the gym*?

❸ Four Kinds of Sentences

A sentence that makes a statement and ends with a period is called a *declarative sentence.*

The baseball game will go extra innings.

A sentence that asks a question and ends with a question mark is called an *interrogative sentence.*

Which team do you think will win?

A sentence that makes a request or gives a command is called an *imperative sentence.*

Please hand me the popcorn.

A sentence that expresses strong emotion and ends with an exclamation point is called an *exclamatory sentence.*

What an exciting game!

═ NOUNS ═

❹ Recognizing Nouns

A noun is the name of a person, place, or thing. A proper noun names a particular person, place, or thing and is always capitalized. All other nouns are common nouns; they are not capitalized.

He climbed the *mountain.*
He climbed *Mount Whitney.*
That *girl* is a scuba diver.
Karen is a scuba diver.

If the proper noun contains more than one word, capitalize all the important words. Do not capitalize a short word such as *of, and,* or *the* unless it is the first word in a title.

Pacific Ocean   The Shining
Dan and Dave's Repair Shop

❺ Abstract and Concrete Nouns

A concrete noun names something that you can see or touch.

boy, Charlie, rock, giraffe, cloud, essay

An abstract noun names a thought, a quality, an idea, or a feeling.

democracy, honesty, delight, theory, pain

❻ Singular and Plural Nouns

Just about every noun has two forms. The singular form names one person, place, or thing.

A *soldier* marched by.
Loyalty is a virtue.

The plural form names more than one person, place, or thing.

The *soldiers* marched by.
His *loyalties* are divided.

❼ Spelling Plural Nouns

Most nouns are made plural by adding *s* to the singular form.

sunflower*s*, oak*s*, porcupine*s*

Nouns that end in *s, ss, ch, sh,* or *x* are made plural by adding *es* to the singular form.

bonus*es*, glass*es*, church*es*, wish*es*, tax*es*

Nouns that end in *y* are made plural in two different ways. If the *y* ending of the singular noun is preceded by a vowel, add *s* to form the plural.

valley / valley*s*   toy / toy*s*

112

If the *y* ending of the singular noun is preceded by a consonant, change the y to *i* and add *es*.

bully / bull*ies*   butterfly / butterfl*ies*

Some nouns that end in *f, fe,* or *ff* are made plural by adding *s*. Others are made plural by changing the *f* to *v* and adding *es*.

staff / sta*ffs*   knife / kni*ves*   half / hal*ves*

There are a number of exceptions to these rules. Always check a dictionary to make sure.

Nouns that end in *o* are made plural in two different ways. When a vowel precedes the *o*, the plural is usually formed by adding *s*. When a consonant precedes the *o*, the plural is usually formed by adding *es*. Check a dictionary to be sure.

studio / stud*ios*   potato / pota*toes*

Some nouns are made plural with a change of internal spelling.

child / *children*   woman / *women*   louse / *lice*

A few nouns are the same in both singular and plural form.

deer / *deer*   moose / *moose*

❽ Possessive Nouns

The possessive form of a noun shows ownership or relationship. A singular noun is made possessive by adding an *apostrophe* and an *s*.

the state*'s* inhabitants
the governor*'s* decision

The possessive form of a singular noun that ends in *s* is made by adding an apostrophe and an *s* or by adding just an apostrophe.

Agne*s's* essay
the bos*s's* office
Mr. Brook*s'* desk

The possessive form of a plural noun that ends in *s* is made by adding just an apostrophe.

the monkey*s'* cages   the student*s'* lockers

❾ Collective Nouns

Collective nouns name groups of people or things. A collective noun that refers to the group as a whole takes a singular verb.

The crowd *was roaring*. Our team *is playing*.

A collective noun that refers to the individual members of the group takes a plural verb.

**The committee *are discussing* their differences.
The jury *were arguing* among themselves.**

❿ Compound Nouns

A compound noun combines two or more words into one. Some compound nouns contain hyphens, but most do not.

sunshine, heartbeat, standard-bearer

Most compound nouns are made plural in the usual ways.

toothbrush*es*, spaceship*s*, sales*men*

To make the plural form, add *s* to the noun in a compound that also contains describing words.

sergeant-at-arms / sergeant*s*-at-arms
hanger-on / hanger*s*-on

⓫ Suffixes That Form Nouns

Certain suffixes make nouns of verbs and adjectives. Some of these suffixes are *dom, ness, er, ster, y, ion, ery, ant,* and *or*.

truthful + *ness* = truthfulness
sail + *or* = sailor

═══ PRONOUNS ═══

⓬ Recognizing Pronouns

Personal pronouns are words used to replace nouns in sentences. The noun the pronoun replaces is called its antecedent. A pronoun must agree with its antecedent in number (singular or plural) and gender (masculine, feminine, or neuter).

We enjoyed the *folktale* because *it* was funny.
Since *Rob* moved away, I miss *him* a lot.
Where is *Martha* when I need *her*?

⓭ Subject and Object Forms of Personal Pronouns

The subject forms of the personal pronouns are *I, you, he, she, it, we,* and *they*.

I drive.	*You* ride.	*She* walks.
It leaks.	*We* applaud.	*They* smile.

The object forms of the personal pronouns are *me, you, him, her, it, us,* and *them*.

Tell *me*.	Help *him*.	Thank *her*.
Join *us*.	Hide *it*.	Follow *them*.

⓮ Reflexive Pronouns

A reflexive pronoun refers back to a noun or pronoun in the same sentence. Reflexive pronouns end in *self* or *selves*.

The dancers looked at *themselves* in the mirror.
Louis must take responsibility for *himself*.

⓯ Possessive Pronouns

Possessive pronouns show ownership or relationship. The following possessive pronouns are used before nouns in sentences: *my, your, his, her, its, our, their.*

my purse	*your* tie	*his* idea
its purpose	*our* home	*their* problem

Possessive pronouns that may not be used before nouns are *mine, yours, his, hers, its, ours, theirs.*

Is the blue bike *his* or is it *hers*?
The tan house is *theirs. Ours* is next door.

Notice that possessive pronouns, unlike possessive nouns, do *not* include an apostrophe.

⓰ Demonstrative Pronouns

Demonstrative pronouns point out persons, places, and things. *This, that, these,* and *those* are demonstrative pronouns. *This* and *these* point out things that are nearby. *That* and *those* indicate things that are farther away.

These are my clothes. *Those* are falling stars.

⓱ Relative Pronouns

Relative pronouns connect a noun or another pronoun with a word group that tells more about it. The relative pronouns are *who, whom, whose, which,* and *that.*

Matt had a flat tire, *which* he had to repair.
The girl *who* lives in Denver represents Colorado.

The relative pronouns *who, whom,* and *whose* refer to people. *Who* is used as a subject, *whom* is used as an object, and *whose* shows ownership or relationship. The relative pronouns *that* and *which* refer to places or things.

⓲ Interrogative Pronouns

Interrogative pronouns are used to ask questions. The interrogative pronouns are *what, which, who, whom,* and *whose.*

Which singer do you like best?
To *whom* are you speaking?

⓳ Indefinite Pronouns

Indefinite pronouns stand on their own because there is usually no specific antecedent.

Is *anybody* here?
Something is missing.
She explained *nothing.*

═ VERBS ═

⓴ Recognizing Verbs

A verb is always part of a sentence's predicate. An action verb expresses physical or mental action.

Kyle *chopped* wood.   Kelly *eats* lunch.

A linking verb expresses what is or seems to be. It links the subject with the predicate.

Wendy *seems* tired.   The debaters *are* ready.

Many linking verbs can also be used as action verbs.

㉑ Subject-Verb Agreement

A verb and its subject must agree in person (I, you, he/she/it), number (singular or plural), and gender (masculine, feminine, or neuter).

I *am* going. (**not:** I *are* going.)
They *play* well. (**not:** They *plays* well.)
Carlos broke *his* wrist.
   (**not:** Carlos broke *her* wrist.)

Some nouns are plural in form, but singular in meaning. Use singular verbs with these words.

Athletics *is* his interest.
   (**not:** Athletics *are* his interest.)

The words *one, each, every, neither, either, everyone, nobody, everybody,* and *somebody* always take a singular verb.

Everyone *is* invited. (**not:** Everyone *are* invited.)

Compound subjects joined by *and* are usually plural. They take a plural verb form.

Dogs and cats *fight*. (**not:** Dogs and cats *fights*.)

Compound subjects joined by *or* are usually singular. They take a singular verb form.

Chocolate or vanilla *is* fine with me.
   (**not:** Chocolate or vanilla *are* fine with me.)

㉒ Verb Tense

A verb's tense shows when it is happening in time (past, present, or future). Verbs change form to show changes in time. The ending *d* or *ed* is usually added to a verb to show past tense. The helping verbs *will* and *shall* are used to express future tense.

Teresa *works.*
Teresa *worked.*
Teresa *will work.*

Verbs that change tense in this predictable way are called regular verbs.

㉓ Irregular Past Tense Verbs

Irregular verbs do not form the past tense with the addition of *d* or *ed*. Instead, they change internal spelling.

grow/*grew*   run/*ran*   tell/*told*   see/*saw*

㉔ Verb Phrases

A verb phrase is made up of two or more verbs that function together in a sentence. The last verb in a verb phrase is the main verb.

We *have enrolled.*   The car *had vanished.*

In a verb phrase, the *ing* ending is used to show continuing action in the present.

They are *voting.*   Mr. Crenshaw is *teaching.*

Action in the past is usually shown by adding *d*, *ed*, *n*, or *en* to the plural form of the main verb. The main verb usually follows a form of the helping verb *have*.

Finally, he *had told* his mother.
He *had dreaded* upsetting her.

A form of the word *do* is often used as a helping verb in a verb phrase.

Why *did* you *scream* like that?
Do you *have* no self-control?

The helping verbs *can, could, may, might, must, should,* and *would* are often used in verb phrases.

Could you *drive*?   I *might join* you.
Must you *leave* early?   I *can stay* later.

㉕ Active and Passive Verb Phrases

In sentences written in the active voice, the subject *performs* the action. In sentences written in the passive voice, the subject *receives* the action. To write in the passive voice, use a form of the helping verb *be* and a past tense verb.

The package *was shipped.*
The actors *were applauded.*

Usually, the passive voice should only be used when the writer doesn't know who or what performed the action. Most good writing is in the active voice.

ADJECTIVES AND ADVERBS

㉖ Recognizing Adjectives

An adjective is a word that describes a noun or pronoun. An adjective usually appears *before* a noun or *after* a linking verb.

Adjectives usually tell *what kind, which one,* or *how many*.

Clever jokes make me laugh.
Elaine's jokes are *hilarious*.

Adjectives that tell *which one* or *how many* always come *before* nouns.

Several students got *perfect* scores.
That student didn't take *this* test.

Adjectives that tell *what kind* can sometimes stand alone.

George felt *discouraged*.
Holly was *delighted*.

㉗ Articles

The words *a, an,* and *the* are special adjectives called articles. They come before nouns in sentences. Use *a* before a word that begins with a consonant. Use *an* before a word that begins with a vowel.

a diploma, *a* school, *an* idea, *an* interview

Use *a* and *an* with singular nouns. *The* is used with both singular and plural nouns.

a bird/*the* birds   *an* elephant/*the* elephants

㉘ Predicate Adjectives

Predicate adjectives often appear after linking verbs. They tell more about the subject noun or pronoun.

The baby *was premature*. His health *is poor*.

㉙ Proper Adjectives

A proper adjective is an adjective formed from a proper noun.

the Denver Mint, Chinese food,
the Victorian era

㉚ Using Adjectives to Compare

Adjectives can be used to compare two or more people or things. The comparative form is used to compare two people or things. To make the comparative form, add *er* to one-syllable adjectives and most two-syllable adjectives.

a great interest/a *greater* interest
a friendly neighbor/a *friendlier* neighbor

Use *more* or *less* before some two-syllable adjectives and before all adjectives with more than two syllables. Check a dictionary if you're not certain of the correct comparative form.

fearful/*more fearful*   desirable/*less desirable*

The superlative form of an adjective is used when more than two people or things are compared. Add *est* to adjectives with one syllable and to many adjectives with two syllables.

> smart/smarter/*smartest*   ugly/uglier/*ugliest*

To make the superlative form, use *most* or *least* before some two-syllable adjectives and all adjectives with more than two syllables. Check a dictionary if you're not certain of the correct superlative form.

> beautiful/more beautiful/*most beautiful*
> intelligent/less intelligent/*least* intelligent

㉛ Irregular Adjective Forms

The comparative and superlative forms of *good*, *bad*, *many*, and *much* are irregular. Study the forms shown in the examples.

> the good news/the *better news*/the *best news*
> a bad result/a *worse result*/the *worst result*
> many chances/*more chances*/*most chances*
> much damage/*more damage*/*most damage*

㉜ Recognizing Adverbs

An adverb is used to describe a verb, an adjective, or another adverb. Adverbs tell *how*, *when*, *where*, or *how often*.

> They arrived *early*.
> The hall filled *quickly*.
> We drove *downtown*.
> The paper is delivered *daily*.

㉝ Adverb Placement

Adverbs that describe verbs can often be placed before or after the verb without changing the sentence's meaning. Adverbs that describe adjectives and adverbs usually are placed before the words they describe.

> He ate *noisily*.
> He *noisily* ate.
> It is *uncomfortably* hot.

㉞ Comparative and Superlative Forms of Adverbs

When no more than two people or things are compared, use the comparative form of the adverb. This form is made by adding *er* to some short adverbs and by adding *more* or *less* before most adverbs.

> She jumps *higher* than I do.
> I got up *earlier* than you did.
> Lou is *more studious* than Sue.
> Sue is *less ambitious* than Lou.

Use the superlative form of an adverb to compare more than two people or things. This form is made by adding *est* to some short adverbs. Use *most* or *least* before most adverbs.

> The *latest* date to apply is July 1.
> Maya is the *most curious* girl I know.
> Neil is the *least courageous* lion tamer.

㉟ Negative Adverbs

Negative adverbs, like *not* and *never*, cancel the action of the verb or deny the state of being. Other negatives are *no*, *no one*, *nobody*, *nothing*, *nowhere*, *none*, *hardly*, *barely*, and *scarcely*.

> You will *not believe* my story.
> I would *never lie* to you, however.

㊱ Avoiding Double Negatives

Use only one negative word in a sentence.

> I had *no* lunch.
> I had *nothing* for lunch.
> I did *not* have anything for lunch.

PREPOSITIONS

㊲ Recognizing Prepositions

A preposition shows the relationship between a noun and other words in a sentence. Some common prepositions are *on*, *in*, *under*, *before*, *behind*, *with*, *without*, *toward*, *over*, and *through*.

> *on* the wall   *over* the bridge   *up* the chimney

㊳ Prepositional Phrases

A preposition is always part of a word group called a prepositional phrase. A prepositional phrase begins with the preposition and ends with a noun or pronoun.

> *upon the shelf   in the house   along the river*

㊴ The Object of the Preposition

The noun or pronoun that follows a preposition is its object.

> We gave a party for *Jared*.
> I hide money beneath my *bed*.

㊵ Personal Pronouns in Prepositional Phrases

A personal pronoun in a prepositional phrase is in the object form. The object forms of personal pronouns are *me*, *you*, *him*, *her*, *it*, *us*, and *them*. Notice that when the object of a preposition is a pronoun, the prepositional phrase usually has only two words.

> I borrowed a pen *from him* and loaned it *to her*.

41 Using Prepositional Phrases as Adjectives

When prepositional phrases describe nouns or pronouns, they do the work of adjectives.

> Bushels *of apples* filled the truck.
> Most students *in our class* buy lunch.

42 Using Prepositional Phrases as Adverbs

When prepositional phrases describe verbs, adjectives, or adverbs, they do the work of adverbs.

> *In 1920*, radio was a high-tech invention.
> Do you live *within walking distance* of school?

43 Prepositional Phrases and Infinitives

The word *to* is sometimes used as part of the infinitive verb form rather than as a preposition. The infinitive form contains the word *to* and the plural form of an action verb.

> *To jump that high* is truly amazing.

CONJUNCTIONS AND INTERJECTIONS

44 Recognizing Conjunctions

A conjunction is a connecting word. Conjunctions are used to join single words, word groups, and sentence parts. The most common conjunctions are *and, but, or, nor, because, although, so, unless*, and *until*.

> I had to wait, *so* I read my book.
> Bananas *and* grapes are my favorite fruits.
> Jake will leave, *unless* you ask him to stay.

45 Subordinating Conjunctions

Subordinating conjunctions connect word groups that are not equal. This kind of conjunction begins a subordinate clause, a group of words that contains a subject and a verb but cannot stand alone as a sentence. When a subordinate clause is joined to a main clause, which can stand alone, a complex sentence is formed.

Subordinate clauses are adverb clauses. They tell *when, where, how,* or *why.*

> Mia runs to her baby *whenever he cries.*
> *Before I fall asleep,* I always say my prayers.

46 Commas with Subordinating Conjunctions

Use a comma after a subordinate clause that begins a sentence.

> *Because of bad weather,* the concert was canceled.

47 Coordinating Conjunctions

A coordinating conjunction joins two equal parts of a sentence. The most common coordinating conjunctions are *and, but,* and *or.*

> Heather is an actress, *and* her brother is her manager.
> Kevin Callahan *or* Mike Perez will raise the flag.
> Joe likes skateboarding, *but* he likes ice skating better.

48 Recognizing Interjections

Interjections are words that express emotion or feeling. A comma separates a mild interjection from the rest of the sentence. An exclamation point is used after an interjection that shows greater excitement.

> *Oh,* it's only you.   *Oh, no!* My car's on fire!

SUBJECTS AND PREDICATES

49 Simple and Complete Subjects

The simple subject in a sentence is its most important noun or pronoun. The object of a preposition *cannot* be the sentence's simple subject.

> The best *sprinter* on the track team is Henry.
> A 12-year-old *girl* rescued the drowning swimmer.

A complete subject includes the simple subject and all other words that are not part of the predicate.

> *Going to school without breakfast* is foolish.

50 Simple and Complete Predicates

The simple predicate in a sentence is the verb or verb phrase.

> Golfer Gary Player *has* always *had* many fans.
> His admirers *follow* him from hole to hole.

A complete predicate includes the simple predicate and all other words that are not part of the subject.

> Merton *believes that regular exercise is essential.*

51 Compound Subjects and Predicates

A compound subject is a combination of two or more subjects used with the same predicate.

> Tetras and angelfish are two of my favorites.

A compound predicate is a combination of two or more predicates used with the same subject.

> Watch them *swim to the surface and gobble their food.*

52 Direct Objects, Indirect Objects, and Predicate Nouns

A direct object is the noun or pronoun that receives the action of the verb.

Jason hit the *ball*. He dropped the *bat* and ran.

An indirect object is the noun or pronoun for whom an action is done.

Shawn gave *me* his coat.

A predicate noun follows a linking verb and renames the subject.

Frederick P. Lawton is the *mayor* of our town.

53 Sentence Fragments and Run-Togethers

A sentence fragment is a group of words capitalized and punctuated as a sentence but lacking an important sentence part.

The child in the blue jacket.
Right after the earthquake.

A run-together is a combination of two sentences incorrectly punctuated as one.

Marcy doesn't like drawing she'd rather paint.

═══ PHRASES AND CLAUSES ═══

54 Recognizing Phrases and Clauses

A clause is a group of words that has a subject and a verb.

until the votes are counted
when the campaign continues

A phrase is a group of words that lacks a subject or a verb.

while voting   *since Easter Sunday*

55 Infinitive and Gerund Phrases

An infinitive phrase can be used as a noun. It begins with an infinitive (the word *to* followed by the plural form of an action verb).

To swim in that creek could be dangerous.
The sweaty children wanted *to cool off*.

A gerund phrase can also be used as a noun. It begins with a gerund (a verb that ends in *ing* and is used as a noun).

Fishing for bass is lots of fun.
We don't mind *releasing the fish* we catch.

56 Phrases Used to Describe

Phrases that function as adjectives tell more about nouns or pronouns. An appositive is a noun or noun phrase that directly follows and explains another noun.

Brenda, *my cousin from New York*, is visiting.
Our senator, *Helen Bradley*, is out of town.

A verb phrase can also function as an adjective. It may begin with a present tense verb ending in *ing*. It might also begin with a past tense verb, such as *seen*.

Waiting for orders, the soldiers stood at attention.

57 Dependent and Independent Clauses

A dependent clause may function as a noun, an adjective, or an adverb within a sentence. It *cannot* stand alone.

After the tornado was over, rescue workers arrived.

An independent, or main, clause can stand alone as a sentence.

The tornado was over.

58 Clauses Used to Describe

An adjective clause, which usually begins with a relative pronoun, describes a noun or a pronoun. The relative pronouns are *who, whose, which, when, that, where,* or *whom.*

Players *who have come to all practices* will make the trip.

Noun clauses can be used as subjects or objects. They usually begin with *who, whose, whoever, why, whomever, which, how, that, what, whatever, when,* and *where.*

Whatever you need will be provided.
Bill can't understand *why Lorna cried*.

An adverb clause tells more about the action verb in a sentence. An adverb clause often begins with a subordinating conjunction. It answers the question *when, where,* or *how.*

Come to my house *before school starts.*

CAPITALIZATION AND PUNCTUATION REFERENCE GUIDE

CAPITALIZATION RULES

❶ First Word in a Sentence

The first word of every sentence begins with a capital letter.

Where are you going?

I'll never tell!

Please take me with you.

❷ First Word in a Direct Quotation

The first word in a direct quotation begins with a capital letter.

"How many states have you visited?" Ken asked.

Jared answered, "I've been in nine states."

If the words a person is speaking are interrupted by other words, do not begin the second part of the quotation with a capital letter.

"Midori," Kelly said, "has visited all 50 states."

❸ Greetings and Closings in Letters

Use a capital letter to begin the first word of a greeting in a letter.

Dear Mrs. Albright:

Dear Aunt Madelene,

Use a capital letter to begin the first word in the closing of a letter.

Sincerely yours,   Cordially,

Best wishes,   Very sincerely,

❹ The Personal Pronoun *I* and Interjection *O*

The personal pronoun *I* and the interjection *O* are both capitalized.

I like Walt Whitman's poem.

You and I will read it.

"O Captain! my captain! our fearful trip is done."

❺ Outlines

Capitalize the first word in all headings of an outline.

I. Job search
  A. Classified ads
    1. Circle good possibilities
    2. Write cover letters
  B. Employment agencies

❻ Proper Nouns

Capitalize all nouns that name a particular person, place, or thing.

Niagara Falls   Library of Congress

Lincoln Memorial   Pacific Ocean

❼ Names and Initials

Capitalize each part of a person's name.

Bo Jackson   Harriet Tubman

Hillary Rodham Clinton   Dana Joy Smithson

Capitalize an initial that is part of a person's name.

J. Barton Kent   Harry S. Truman

❽ Personal and Professional Titles

Capitalize a title that is used before a person's name.

Rev. Jesse Jackson

President George Washington

Ms. Gloria Steinem

Senator Barbara Boxer

❾ Titles of Relationship

Capitalize family titles that are used as names or parts of names.

Uncle Pete   Grandma Helen   Mom

Usually, if a possessive pronoun comes before a family title, do not begin that word with a capital letter.

my cousin Lucy   her aunt Grace

❿ Nationalities and Languages

Begin the names of nationalities and languages with a capital letter.

my French class   the British people

Belgian chocolate   a Swiss watch

⓫ Names of Cities and Towns

Capitalize each word in the name of a city or town.

Oklahoma City   Grover's Corners   St. Louis

⓬ Names of Streets and Highways

Capitalize each word in the name of a street or highway.

Laurel Avenue

Green Valley Boulevard

Old Bayshore Road

Long Island Expressway

⑬ Names of States, Countries, and Continents

Capitalize each word in the name of a state, country, or continent.

Antarctica	South Africa	Portugal
Europe	New Zealand	North America

⑭ Geographic Names

Capitalize each word in the name of a geographic place.

Mount Hood
Yellowstone National Park
the Red Sea
Carlsbad Caverns

⑮ Proper Adjectives

A proper adjective is formed from a proper noun. It describes a particular person, place, or thing. Capitalize each word in a proper adjective.

a Scandinavian buffet
a Martin Scorsese film
a Stephen King novel
West Indian fashions

⑯ Direction Words

Capitalize compass directions that refer to particular geographical areas.

Come to the Northeast.
We've always lived down South.

Do not capitalize a direction word used as a common adjective before a noun.

Do you like southern food?
Idaho is a western state.

⑰ Brand Names

Capitalize the brand names of products.

Goodrich milk
Warm-U furnaces
Sudso soap

⑱ Organizations and Religions

Capitalize the main words in the names of organizations.

Department of Commerce
Campfire Girls
Boys and Girls Clubs of America

Capitalize the names of religions and their followers.

Presbyterians	Catholicism

⑲ Titles of Works

Capitalize the first word, the last word, and every important word in the title of a work. Except at the beginning of a title, the words *a, an,* and *the* are not capitalized. Prepositions with fewer than five letters and coordinating conjunctions are not capitalized.

The Wreck of the Hesperus
Romeo and Juliet
Whistler's Mother
The Ransom of Red Chief

⑳ Days, Months, and Holidays

Begin the names of days, months, and holidays with capital letters.

July	Wednesday	Independence Day

═══ PUNCTUATION RULES ═══

㉑ Period at the End of a Sentence

Use a period at the end of a declarative sentence. (A declarative sentence is one that makes a statement.)

The earthquake scared everyone.
Much damage was done.

Use a period at the end of an imperative sentence. (An imperative sentence gives a command.)

Be here at 8 o'clock.
Bring your sleeping bag.

㉒ Question Mark at the End of a Sentence

Use a question mark at the end of an interrogative sentence. (An interrogative sentence asks a question.)

Where is your sister?
When will she be home?

㉓ Exclamation Point at the End of a Sentence

Use an exclamation point at the end of an exclamatory sentence. (An exclamatory sentence expresses surprise or excitement.)

What a great performance!
I got his autograph!

㉔ Periods with Abbreviations

Use a period at the end of most abbreviations. Usually, titles used before people's names are abbreviated.

Mr. Currier	Dr. Li	Ms. Zelinski

Abbreviations of government agencies, labor unions, and certain other organizations are not completed with periods.

CIA   FBI   AFL   NBC

25 Periods with Initials

Use a period after an initial that is part of a person's name.

John F. Kennedy   B. J. Hunnicutt

26 Commas in a Series

Use commas to separate the words or groups of words in a series. (A series is a group of three or more words or groups of words that are used the same way in a sentence.)

Slice two apples, two oranges, and two bananas.

Dan invited Ed, Mark, Eric, Tod, and Smitty.

27 Commas in Dates

Use a comma between the number of the day and the number of the year in a date.

July 4, 1776   January 1, 2000

If the date appears at the beginning or in the middle of a sentence, use another comma after the year.

December 7, 1941, was a day of infamy.

Do not use a comma if the date includes only the month and the year.

They moved to Chicago in September 1995.

Do not use a comma if the date includes only the month and the day.

May 5 is the anniversary of Mexican independence.

28 Commas in Addresses

Use a comma between the name of a city or town and the name of a state or country.

Phoenix, Arizona

Bogotá, Colombia

Use another comma after the state or country if the two words come at the beginning or in the middle of a sentence.

Lincoln, Nebraska, is the home of the Cornhuskers.

We visited Paris, France, after we left London.

29 Commas in Compound Sentences

Use a comma before the conjunction in a compound sentence. (The coordinating conjunctions are *or, nor, and, but.*)

Many were injured, but no one was killed.

We can wait for the bus, or we can walk home.

30 Commas After Introductory Phrases and Clauses

Use a comma after a phrase that comes before the subject of a sentence. (A phrase is a group of words that usually functions as an adjective or adverb.)

Upon the highest peak, the mountain climbers rested.

Use a comma after an adverb clause at the beginning of a sentence.

A few minutes after dawn, the fish started biting.

31 Commas after Introductory Words

Use a comma to set off introductory words like *yes* and *no,* and mild exclamations.

No, I can't attend.   Yes, I won the prize.
Oh, he doesn't care.   Well, that's all right.

Use a comma to set off words of direct address.

Maggie, you're up next.   Nice going, Billie!

If a noun of address appears in the middle of a sentence, use commas before and after the noun.

My neighbor, Felix Vargas, is a pilot.

32 Commas with Appositives

Use a comma before an appositive at the end of a sentence. (An appositive is a noun or noun phrase that explains another noun.)

Marty and I enjoy the same sport, tennis.

An appositive that appears in the middle of a sentence is set off with commas on each side.

Johnny Weismuller, the first Tarzan, is my favorite.

33 Commas to Set Off Separate Thoughts or Explanations

Use a comma to set off a separate thought or explanation at the end of a sentence. If the separate part comes in the middle of the sentence, use a comma before and after it.

It is very hot in the summer in Sacramento, the capital of California.

Sacramento, the capital of California, is very hot in the summer.

34 Apostrophes to Show Ownership

The possessive form of a singular noun is shown by adding an apostrophe and an *s*.

Ron's motorcycle   the coach's whistle

The possessive form of a plural noun that ends in *s* is shown by adding only an apostrophe.

glasses' lenses   farmers' crops

Add an apostrophe and an *s* to show the possessive form of a plural noun that does not end in *s*.

women's dresses   oxen's tracks

35 Apostrophes for Missing Letters

In a contraction, use an apostrophe in place of the missing letter or letters.

cannot—can't

Mandy is—Mandy's

I would—I'd

36 Quotation Marks for Direct Quotations

Use quotation marks at the beginning and at the end of a direct quotation. (A direct quotation is the exact words a person said.)

"Neither a borrower nor a lender be," advised Benjamin Franklin.

37 Quotation Marks with Titles of Works

Use quotation marks around the title of a story, poem, song, essay, or chapter.

Our class just read "The Outcasts of Poker Flat."

The choir sang "The Battle Hymn of the Republic."

38 Colons After Greetings in Business Letters

After a greeting in a business letter, use a colon instead of a comma.

Dear Judge O'Connor:

Dear Sir or Madam:

39 Colons in Expressions of Time

Use a colon between the hour and the minutes when you use numerals to write time.

9:30 A.M.   10:15 P.M.

40 Colons Before Lists of Appositives

Use a colon to introduce a list of appositives at the end of a sentence.

There were four members Lisa had not met: Carla, Elizabeth, Mary, and Terry.

41 Colons Before Long, Quoted Passages

Use a colon to introduce a long quotation or a formal statement.

The keynote speaker spoke as follows:
   (Here follows the speaker's words.)

The defense attorney began her summation:
   (Here follows the summarizing speech.)

42 Semicolons to Express Close Relationship

Although the semicolon is the equivalent of a period, it is used to achieve a closer relationship of ideas than a period allows.

You go first; I will follow right behind.

Katie finally found her lost dog; he was in the park.

43 Semicolons with Independent Clauses

Use a semicolon to join independent clauses linked by a conjunctive adverb.

The team got off to a bad start; consequently, they had trouble catching up.

We've had lots of rain; nevertheless, the crops have been disappointing.

Use a semicolon to precede coordinating conjunctions joining independent clauses that are in direct contrast.

I have all the questions; but only you have the answers.

I have many wonderful friends; but none of them want to go to the movies with me.

44 Semicolons in a Series

Use semicolons to prevent misreading of a complicated series.

Among those attending were Mrs. Louanna Wright, our school's principal; Dr. Harry Ford, the superintendent of our school district; Ms. Alice Kelly, a curriculum specialist; and Reuben Lopez, the president of the student council.

45 Hyphens to Join or Separate Words

The hyphen is used only in specific circumstances. It is used to join compound numbers from twenty-one to ninety-nine and fractions used as adjectives.

thirty-six   eighty-eight   a two-thirds majority

The hyphen is used with the prefixes *self, ex,* and *all.* It is also used with all prefixes before a proper noun, a proper adjective, or the name of an office.

self-confident   ex-football player
all-American   mid-August
pro-Israeli   post-World War II

The hyphen is used to prevent confusion.

re-creation *(to distinguish from* recreation*)*

always-to-be-remembered *(to ensure recognition as a single word)*

The hyphen is used to join some compound nouns.

bull's-eye   cure-all   forget-me-not

The hyphen is used to join compound adjectives that precede the nouns they modify.

double-breasted coat   half-dollar raise

When a whole word won't fit on a line, a hyphen is used to show that the word has been separated and will be completed on the next line.

Fourscore and seven years ago our fa-
thers brought forth on this continent

46 The Dash to Show Change of Thought

Use a dash to indicate an abrupt directional change or interruption of thought.

My Aunt Meg—she is my mother's youngest sister—will be a bridesmaid at my wedding.

It may be possible to join you—no, on second thought there is no way I could make it.

Use a dash to emphasize an appositive or to set off a repetition or summary.

Professional athletes—so often the envy of young boys—may be unreliable role models.

Maude, Hazel, Gertrude, Mabel—all of these were popular names in 1900.

47 The Ellipsis to Show Omission

Three spaced dots called *points of ellipsis* show where words have been left out. Using an ellipsis may leave a grammatical structure incomplete, but it does not affect the meaning of a sentence.

Children need . . . a sense of security.

When an ellipsis occurs at the end of a declarative sentence, the three points of ellipsis are followed by a period.

The cookies were fresh and Mike was hungry, so . . . .

48 The Slash

A slash can be used to indicate a choice between two contradictory options.

No grades are given in study skills class. It is a pass/fail course.

Slashes are used to indicate line breaks when a poem is quoted in the text of a paper.

'Twas the night before Christmas, when all through the house/Not a creature was stirring—not even a mouse!/The stockings were hung by the chimney with care

49 Parentheses to Set Apart Information

Use parentheses to enclose various types of material that are not essential to a sentence or paragraph but may be informative to the reader.

Parentheses are used when an editorial comment is made.

He traveled 100 miles (what a grueling walk!) to get help.

Parentheses are used with an enlargement on preceding material.

He made a fortune (more than a million, some claim) on his simple invention.

Parentheses are used in a translation.

At last it was *buenos noches* (good night) for all of us.

Parentheses are used around letters or numerals listed in a sentence or paragraph.

Any good speech has been: (1) thoroughly researched, (2) carefully organized, (3) well rehearsed, and (4) revised to maximum perfection.

Parentheses are used to ensure mathematical accuracy.

Enclosed is my personal check for eleven dollars and sixty-four cents ($11.64).

50 Brackets for Clarification

Brackets are inserted in a quoted passage to explain, comment, or correct.

"He was born in 1805 [actually, in 1803] in Paris."

"It [Moby Dick] was finally published in 1851."

SPELLING REFERENCE GUIDE

❶ Consonants and Vowels

Consonants are speech sounds that block or partly block the breath with the tongue, teeth, or lips. All the letters of the alphabet, *except a, e, i, o, u,* and sometimes *y* are consonants.

Vowels are speech sounds made by using the voice without blocking the breath with the tongue, teeth, or lips. The letters that make vowel sounds are *a, e, i, o, u,* and sometimes *y.*

❷ Consonant Clusters

Consonant clusters are groups of two or more letters that make a single sound. Consonant clusters appear in many English words.

ri**ch**, pa**tch**, **wh**ere, **sh**ed, so**ng**

❸ Short Vowels

Short vowel sounds are made with a quick flow of breath.

c**a**p, s**e**t, n**i**p, h**o**p, c**u**p

❹ Long Vowels

Long vowel sounds are the same as the name of the letter. These sounds are made with a longer flow of breath.

c**a**ke, m**ee**t, k**i**te, h**o**pe, m**u**le, cr**y**

❺ Long *a* Sound

Long *a* may be spelled *a, ai,* or *ei.*

f**a**de, g**ai**n, **ei**ghty

❻ Long *e* Sound

Long *e* may be spelled *e, ea, ee, ei, ie,* or *y.*

b**e**cause, t**ea**m, w**ee**p, dec**ei**ve, th**ie**f, onl**y**

❼ Long *i* Sound

Long *i* may be spelled *i, ie, igh,* or *y.*

r**i**pe, p**ie**, f**igh**t, fr**y**

❽ Long *o* Sound

Long *o* may be spelled *o, oa, ow,* or *ough.*

t**o**ne, b**oa**t, gl**ow**, d**ough**

❾ Long *u* Sound

Long *u* may be spelled *u, eu, ew, iew, o, oo, ou, ue,* or *ui.*

c**u**te, f**eu**d, st**ew**, v**iew**, d**o**, t**oo**l, s**ou**p, gl**ue**, br**ui**se

❿ Homophones

Homophones are words that sound alike but have different meanings and different spellings. A mistakenly chosen homophone appears to be a spelling error.

die/dye   for/four   which/witch   your/you're

⓫ Prefixes

A prefix is one or more syllables joined to the beginning of a base word or root to change its meaning. The spelling of a word does not change when a prefix is added.

PREFIX	MEANING	EXAMPLES
un	not	*uneventful unlimited*
in	not	*ineffective inactive*
il	not	*illegible illogical*
im	not	*improper immature*
ir	not	*irreversible irresistible*
de	off, away from	*deport deemphasize*
dis	away from, out of	*discharge disgrace*
mis	wrong, wrongly	*misunderstand mispronounce*
inter	among, between	*interview interact*
sub	under, less than	*subtract submerge*
per	through, by	*perforate perjure*
pro	before, favoring	*proclaim pronounce*
pre	before, ahead	*preheat predict*

Dozens of additional prefixes are used in hundreds of words. Some of these prefixes are *anti, auto, cent, tele, tri, under, semi, mono, uni, kilo, milli, mega, micro, hypo,* and *hyper.*

12 Suffixes

A suffix is a syllable or group of syllables added to the end of a base word or root to change its meaning. Some suffixes change the spelling of the original word.

13 Suffix: *ly*

The suffix *ly* makes an adverb of an adjective.

slow**ly**, kind**ly**, quick**ly**

14 Suffixes: *ful, less*

You will not usually change a word's spelling when you add *ful* or *less*.

dread**ful**, care**ful**   sense**less**, care**less**

If the base word ends in *y*, however, change the *y* to *i* before adding *ful* or *less*.

duti**ful**, beauti**ful**   penni**less**, merci**less**

15 Suffixes: *ise, ize*

These suffixes turn nouns into verbs. Although there are no rules to help you decide between these spellings, many more words end in *ize* than *ise*.

advert**ise**   memor**ize**

16 Suffixes: *ant, ance, ancy, ent, ence, ency*

These suffixes turn verbs into nouns. There are no rules to help you choose between the *a* or *e* spellings. As with other suffixes, however, you must first drop the base word's final *e* or change the final *y* to *i*.

pleas**ant**, signific**ance**, tru**ancy**, excell**ent**, pati**ence**, emerg**ency**

17 Suffixes: *ed, t, ing*

The word endings *ed* and *t* show the past tense form of a verb. The *ing* ending shows ongoing action in the present. Only a few verbs form the past tense with *t*.

mean**t**, slep**t**

Drop the verb's final *e* before adding *ed* or *ing*.

smil**ed**, smil**ing**

Usually, if the verb ends in *y*, change the *y* to *i* before adding *ed*. Do *not* change the *y* before adding *ing*.

worri**ed**, worry**ing** (Exceptions are words like *played, enjoyed, stayed*.)

18 Suffix: *ous*

This suffix turns a noun into an adjective. In most words, the noun's spelling does not change.

poison**ous**, mountain**ous**

If the noun ends in *f*, however, change the *f* to *v* before adding *ous*.

mischie**vous**, grie**vous**

Usually, you will drop a noun's final *e* before adding *ous*.

ridicul**ous**, nerv**ous**

If the noun ends in *ge*, however, you will *not* drop the *e*.

courage**ous**, outrage**ous**

If the noun ends in *ce*, change the *e* to *i* before adding *ous*.

graci**ous**, spaci**ous**

19 Suffixes: *er, est*

These suffixes make comparisons when added to adjectives or adverbs. They show *more* and *most*.

small**er**, small**est**   rich**er**, rich**est**

As you do before adding other suffixes, first change the base word's *y* to *i*.

friendli**er**, friendli**est**   angri**er**, angri**est**

20 Suffixes: *tion, sion*

These word endings turn verbs into nouns. Before adding these suffixes, you will often change the spelling of the base word.

If the base word ends in *se* or *te*, drop the *e* before adding *tion*.

educate/educa**tion**   tense/ten**sion**

If the base word ends in *ce*, drop the *e* before adding *ion*.

produce/produc**tion**   deduce/deduc**tion**

If the base word ends in *t*, add *ion*.

act/act**ion**   reflect/reflect**ion**

If the base word ends in *ss*, add *ion*.

confess/confess**ion**   aggress/aggress**ion**

If the base word ends in *d* or *de*, drop the *d* or *de* and add *sion*.

conclude/conclu**sion**   extend/exten**sion**

Some base words end in *a__e* or *i__e*. With these words, you drop the *e* and add *ation*.

separate/separ**ation**   organize/organiz**ation**

21 Suffixes: *ary, ery*

Only a few words end in *ery*.

cemetery, very, stationery

To be certain, you should always check a dictionary. But most words that end in this sound contain the *ary* spelling.

secretary, necessary, temporary

22 Suffixes: *able, ible*

A noun that ends in *ation* becomes an adjective when you add *able*.

demonstration/demonstrable
explanation/explainable

A noun that ends in *ion* becomes an adjective with *ible*.

division/divisible
comprehension/comprehensible

The letters *ss* are usually followed by *ible*.

permissible, admissible

Although many more words end in *able* than *ible*, it is always best to check a dictionary.

23 Suffixes: *er, or, ian*

These three suffixes name a person who *does* something. Some change verbs into nouns. Usually, the spelling of the base word does not change.

player, doctor, musician

If the verb ends in *e*, drop the final *e* before adding *er*.

writer, faker, biker

Dozens of additional suffixes are used in many hundreds of words. Some of these suffixes are *ist, ism, ity, itis, like, mony, ose, phobia, ology*, and *ward*.

24 Words with *ie/ei*

The old rule for deciding which letter comes first will usually be helpful:

***I* before *e* except after *c*, or when sounded like *a* as in neighbor or weigh.**

thief, belief, receive, receipt, eight, veil

When the *c* is pronounced *sh*, however, it may be followed by *ie*.

efficient, conscience

25 Regular and Irregular Plurals

Singular nouns are made plural to show more than one. Usually, a noun is made plural when *s* is added.

toys, boats, governments

Nouns that end in *s, ss, sh, x, ch,* or *z* are made plural by adding *es*.

gases, glasses, dishes, bunches, taxes, buzzes

Some nouns that end in the long *o* sound are made plural by adding *es*.

potatoes, torpedoes

But other nouns that end in long *o* are made plural by adding only an *s*. To be sure, check a dictionary.

pianos, rodeos

Nouns that end in *f* or *fe* are made plural by dropping the *f* or *fe* and adding *ves*.

knife/knives   loaf/loaves   shelf/shelves
Some exceptions to this rule are *roofs, chiefs, beliefs, staffs*.

Nouns that end in *y* are made plural in two ways. If the letter before the *y* is a consonant, drop the *y* and add *ies*.

city/cities   penny/pennies   story/stories

If the letter before the *y* is a vowel, just add *s*.

trolleys, trays, journeys

Some irregular plurals are *teeth, feet, men, women, children, mice,* and *sheep*.

26 The *aw* Sound

This sound can be spelled *a, o, au,* or *aw*.

ball, off, cause, paw

27 The *air* Sound

This sound can be spelled *ar, er, air, are,* or *ear*.

area, very, chair, share, bear

28 The *uh* Sound

This sound can be spelled with any of the five vowels.

alive, often, magnify, atom, hum

29 The *uhl* Sound

This sound can be spelled *le, al,* or *el*.

needle, loyal, level

30 The *ur* Sound

This sound can be spelled *ur, er, ir, or,* or *ar.*

b**ur**n, f**er**n, g**ir**l, w**or**k, sug**ar**

31 The *oi* Sound

This sound can be spelled *oy* or *oi.*

t**oy**, c**oi**n

32 The *ow* Sound

This sound can be spelled *ow* or *ou.*

g**ow**n, cl**ou**d

33 The *oo* Sound

This sound can be spelled *oo, u,* or *ou.*

st**oo**d, f**u**ll, c**ou**ld

34 Words with *ough*

This confusing spelling is pronounced in six different ways. Always use a dictionary to doublecheck words with this spelling.

r**ough**, thr**ough**, thor**ough**, b**ough**, d**ough**, b**ough**t

35 Words with *augh, igh*

The *augh* spelling is pronounced *aw.* The *igh* spelling is pronounced with the long *i* sound.

t**augh**t, s**igh**t

36 Words with *cede, ceed, sede*

These letter combinations are all pronounced *seed.*

pro**ceed**, re**cede**, super**sede**

37 Words with *qu*

The *qu* spelling is pronounced *kw.*

queen, **qu**iet, s**qu**int

38 Words with *ch, tch*

Both spellings make the *ch* sound you hear in *chop.* After a long vowel sound, use *ch.* After a short vowel sound, use *tch.*

pea**ch**, coa**ch**　　ba**tch**, fe**tch**

After a consonant, use *ch.*

in**ch**, lun**ch**

At the beginning of a word, always use *ch.*

champion, **ch**allenge

39 Words with *j, g, ge, dge*

The *j* sound in *joy* can be spelled in all four ways. Before the vowels *a, o,* and *u,* use the *j* spelling.

jam, **j**ob, **j**uice

At the end of a word, the *j* sound is almost always spelled *ge* or *dge.* Use *ge* after a long vowel sound or a consonant. Use *dge* after a short vowel sound.

a**ge**, hu**ge**　　ju**dge**, e**dge**

40 Words with *ph*

In some words the *f* sound is made with the letters *ph.* There are no rules to help you with this spelling. You will have to check a dictionary if you're not sure.

gra**ph**ic, paragra**ph**, tele**ph**one

41 Silent Letters: *l, k, b, w, h*

Silent *l* is usually followed by a consonant. Silent *k* nearly always comes at the beginning of a word and is usually followed by *n.* Silent *b* most often comes after *m* or before *t.* Silent *w* usually comes at the beginning of a word and is followed by *h* or *r.* Silent *h* appears at the beginning of a word or after a consonant.

fo**l**k, **k**nock, lam**b**, **w**ring, **h**our, g**h**oul

42 Silent Letters: *c, n, e, t, g*

Silent *c* usually follows *s.* Silent *n* always appears after *m.* Silent *e* usually appears at the end of a word that has a long vowel sound. Silent *t* usually follows *f* or *s.* Silent *g* most often appears before *n.*

s**c**ience, autum**n**, bik**e**, hus**t**le, champa**g**ne

43 *C* with the Sound of *s/k*

Usually, the *s* sound in a word is spelled *s.* But the *s* sound may be spelled with either an *s* or a *c* when it appears before *e, i,* or *y.* After a long vowel sound, the *s* sound is spelled with *c.*

inno**c**ent, in**c**ident　　spi**c**e, tra**c**e

Most often, the *k* sound in a word is spelled *k* or *ck.* But there are many words in which *c* makes the *k* sound.

criminal, mi**c**rophone, ta**c**ti**c**s, **c**olor

Check a dictionary if you're not sure how to spell the *k* sound in a word.

44 The Apostrophe

An apostrophe followed by *s* is used to show ownership or possession with singular nouns.

Tanya**'s** dress   student**'s** locker

An apostrophe is used to show the plurals of letters, numbers, symbols, abbreviations, and words used as illustrations.

A**'s**   9**'s**   &**'s**   Ph.D.**'s**   and**'s** and but**'s**

With plural nouns that end in s, ownership or possession is shown by placing the apostrophe after the s.

delegates**'** votes   contestants**'** prizes

An apostrophe is used to show where one or more letters have been omitted in a contraction.

we**'ve**   they**'d**   I**'ll**

An apostrophe is used to show where numbers have been omitted.

the roaring **'**20**'**s   the **'**99 Cadillac

45 Abbreviations

Abbreviations are short ways of writing words or phrases. Abbreviations are used to save time, space, and energy. Most abbreviations are followed by a period.

Market **St.**   **Mrs.** Perez   10 **P.M.**

Some common abbreviations are *not* punctuated with periods.

UN   mph   USA

Official U.S. postal abbreviations are used for the 50 states. Each of these abbreviations is spelled with two capital letters without final periods.

NY   CA   IL

46 The Hyphen

A hyphen is used in compound numbers from 21 to 99.

twenty-one   forty-seven

A hyphen is used in fractions used as adjectives.

two-thirds majority   **one-half** interest

A hyphen always follows the prefixes *self, ex,* and *all*.

All-American   **self**-respect   **ex**-convict

A hyphen is always used with prefixes before a proper noun, a proper adjective, or the name of an office.

mid-July   **pro**-Israeli   **ex**-governor

Hyphens are used to connect some compound words.

**sister-in-law   great-grandmother
long-winded   open-minded**